Father
to the
Fatherless

Your Heavenly Father Sees, Hears, and Cares

ESOSA VICTOR OSAI

To my Heavenly Father Yahuah Elohim: I want to see your Kingdom come, and I want to see your will be done! Be a Father to the Fatherless, and a Defender of Widows in this generation. Change this earth for your Glory through your Son Jesus!

To my earthly father Uwaifo Osaigbovo: even though you lost your own father at a young age, you were an amazing Daddy to me. Your integrity, humility, compassion, discipline, and counsel are an amazing and beautiful example to this day!

To my mother Rebecca Osaigbovo: it was your example that inspired me to believe for and seek prayer and revival in the Body of Christ. Thank you for helping to make me who I am today.

To my wife Shereena: Thank you so much for your partnership and companionship. Your fear of YAH and your willingness to obey Him inspire me to be a better man.

To Champion: You are mighty and strong, and Yah will fight for you, so enjoy His presence every day, and have fun!

To Arrow: You are a mighty weapon in Yah's hand. He will protect you, and you will both see and do amazing things!

To Justice: Your heart is a treasure. Keep loving Yah and loving the people you see. Yah will do mighty things through you.

To Lily: Your words have power, and Yah is watching your mouth to do your heart's desire. Your faith will change the world around you!

To Liberty: You were sent by Yah to shine and bring light to everyone around you. We enjoy your presence because you bring God's presence!

To Onyx: You are truly a mighty man of Elohim! We can't wait to hear what He puts inside of your heart!

Contents

Introduction

was very excited when my wife was getting ready to have our first son, Champion. I was looking forward to teaching him the Bible, Business, and Basketball and I told my wife well ahead of time!

We had a home birth that had a couple of adverse events. First, his shoulder was stuck and the midwives had to work feverishly to get him out.

Next, he had breathing issues with fluid in his lungs. We ended up having to rush him to the hospital in an ambulance the day after he was born at home. He was in the NICU for three days.

So, our "home birth" didn't go exactly as expected, but it wasn't until years later that we grasped how serious both of those situations could have been if either of them went the wrong way.

There are people with a permanently disconnected shoulder from being stuck in the birth canal. We didn't even know but the midwives had to execute several procedures to get him out and prevent him and my wife from permanent injuries.

If we hadn't noticed his breathing trouble and called the midwife again, he might not even be here now.

Despite those two situations that could have gone terribly wrong, God had His hand on our firstborn and we are so thankful!

We were ignorant and unexperienced first-time parents, but our Father in Heaven was a father to us all. He surrounded us with wisdom and help.

Not to mention we were "broke as a joke."

I was in between careers when we got married. In the year that Champion was born, our ministry was transitioning from Christian Entertainment to 100% prayer and Biblical Discipleship. We had received some serious warnings from God, so it was a very necessary transition. It was tough financially, and our new ministry was very unpopular.

I remember when Champion had just turned one year old and we went to get our taxes done. He was at the cute stage where he was saying a few of his first words, "Dank too" (thank you) to strangers. Our tax preparer was very charmed by our little boy. At the end of the meeting, we were shocked to find out our taxable income for the entire year was only $16,790! Our income was at an all-time low.

Not to mention, after a year and a half of birth control, we had decided to give God the birth control over our family. We decided to let Him decide when and how many children we would have. Our faith was strong and we believed God for the for financial increase through my work to provide. Now here we were, two years after making that decision, making less than we ever had before. My wife and I just had to look at each other and laugh! Champion's "Dank too" was definitely the highlight of that meeting!

This was a time of great difficulty for me. I was facing the pressure of providing for a family and keeping a marriage together which was very hard for me as a first-time father. I was also being squeezed by betrayal, as ministry partners I trusted turned on me. I was wounded and depressed, crying out to God for answers for the many problems coming at me all at once.

But my Father in heaven was a father to me. He surrounded me with wisdom and help.

This book is written to share with you some of the wisdom and help that God has given me.

God is a Father to the Fatherless!

Your Heavenly Father SEES

- He sees what HAS happened and what IS happening.
- He also knows what SHOULD BE happening, and how to fix it, mend it, and restore it.

Your Heavenly Father HEARS

- He will answer when you call Him.
- He will listen to you and respond.
- You must be ready to listen to His instructions when He answers you.

Your Heavenly Father CARES

- Not only does God have knowledge and wisdom, He is also a compassionate Healer of the brokenhearted.
- He heals and delivers those that have been abused and oppressed.
- He delivers those who suffer inner turmoil from wounds, and will remove the demons (devils) that enter into those wounds.

As you read each chapter, please make sure to go through the **Restoration Steps…**and don't forget to pray the **Restoration Prayers** at the end of the book.

This book is not meant to only be healing to those who have suffered fatherlessness, it's also meant to build up your soul in the Scripture. This is very important.

If we go through healing and deliverance without filling our souls with the knowledge of God, then there is a potential risk for the devil to come back seven times stronger. We must eliminate that risk by walking in obedience to the knowledge of the Truth.

This book is meant to give you the Most High's perspective on the relationships that He designed. It is based on the Living Word of Elohim our Creator.

This is not only a book of liberating truth; it's also a book of deliverance and healing.

With this knowledge, healing, and deliverance, God can restore our hearts, and we can help Him restore all things in this generation.

Chapter 1

Father to the Fatherless: RESTORE YOUR HEART!

grew up in a stable and godly household. I'm very thankful to God that I don't have any abandonment or abuse stories.

I know people with much more horrible stories; who overcame many adversities in their childhoods, and many of their lives have been turned all the way around for God's glory. But by God's grace, I was blessed with a good earthly father that taught, served, and led by example in our home. He was strict on education and on teaching Scriptural values, and he kept covenant faithfulness with my mother. He supported us all in every way. He was our source, and still is a true "abba."

My heart still pours out compassion for those that weren't blessed the same way I was. I see the results of neglect and abuse in our culture every day.

To whom much is given, much is required. I know that one of my requirements from the Most High is to bring healing, deliverance, and restoration to a generation impacted by adultery, divorce, abandonment, abuse, and all forms of fatherlessness.

Fathers can play such a vital role in the life of their children if they are willing to.

Fathers can set the course for the lives of their children and call out their purpose. A lack of this guidance and leadership can cause long lasting damage in a person's life.

Here are some things a father on earth provides:

- Protection
- Resources
- Affection
- Supervision
- Training
- Correction

If we are in Christ, we can also develop a close relationship with our Father in heaven. He is the one who teaches us how to be good earthly fathers. He is our leader and example.

What does your Father in Heaven Provide?

All of the above, plus:

+ Forgiveness
+ Repentance
+ Healing
+ Deliverance
+ Restoration from your past sins.

It is a wonderful blessing to have a father on earth, and a Father in heaven. Everything we need in our lives can potentially come from our fathers. When fatherhood is absent, we could potentially lose every one of those benefits and blessings.

This is why fatherlessness is one of the most destructive forces throughout history of humanity. The loss of guidance and the suffering that it causes can compound among generations when it is unchecked. One pain-filled generation leads to another, and the patterns continue until someone takes responsibility for healing and restoration.

Whatever your earthly father lacked or failed to give you, there is still hope for full restoration. The Scriptures promise us that if we follow Him, our Father in Heaven will take full responsibility for us!

> *Psalms 27:10 When my father and my mother forsake me, then **the Lord will take me up***.

Everyone Suffers Some Degree of Fatherlessness

There are many fathers that didn't know any better, because they were fatherless themselves. There are many fathers that did the best they could, but they didn't have a lot of training or a good example to follow.

Everyone has suffered different levels of fatherlessness. Even if you had a father that lived with you in the home, he probably wasn't perfect. Every human father makes mistakes. Every human father sins. Every human father has work trips that he can't take his family on. Every human father eventually dies.

Even a good father cannot be perfect. The Scripture teaches that even a good father on earth is evil in comparison to God the Father in Heaven (Matthew 7:11).

We all know what being a bad father looks like. We also inherently know what a good father looks like, even if he's not perfect.

The Scriptures confirm: a good earthly father is (1) **there** and (2) **cares**.

A good father **cares** by **desiring your heart**. A good father also is **there** to let you **observe his lifestyle**.

> *Proverbs 23:26 "Give me your **heart**,*
> *let your **eyes observe my ways**."*

Every Degree of Fatherlessness is either a level of (1) not being there or (2) not caring:

- Present but absent emotionally
- Present but unfaithful or sinful
- Present but abusive
- Present but perverted or twisted
- Absent but seeks a relationship
- Absent and evil, a liar
- Dead or deceased

REPAIRING THE BREACH

Everyone on earth will experience a certain degree of fatherlessness at some point, even if it's as an adult and your father passes away into the next life before you do. No earthly father is immortal. Whenever your father dies, you will be fatherless on earth.

Whether you experience fatherlessness at a young age or at an adult old age, you must be prepared spiritually.

The reason we have to be prepared for fatherlessness is that every degree of fatherlessness has the potential to create a wound in our spirit.

A breach (open wound) in a human spirit creates an entryway for unclean spirits (devils, a.k.a. demons), which then creates a perverse tongue.

> *Proverbs 15:4 A wholesome tongue is a tree of life:*
> *but **perverseness** therein is a **breach in the spirit**.*

What's in our hearts comes out of our mouths. When our hearts are healed and whole, we speak good words full of grace and truth. When our hearts are bitter and wounded, we speak curses, negativity, and sin into our atmosphere.

When we cannot stop perverse, bitter, disobedient, unforgiving, unfaithful, or rebellious words from coming from our tongue, we must pray to God that He would **heal our spirit**, put it back together, and show us His love for us.

Your spiritual identity and confidence can be in Him—your Father in Heaven—not in what has happened to you or the things that go on around you!

If you have been wounded, you must verbally forgive those that did you wrong. Then, give God thanks for what you have.

Jesus Christ, the Savior of all men taught that we must forgive each other 70x7=490 times per day! That means every time you think of somebody that did you wrong, you must verbally express forgiveness to keep your heart free from bitterness.

Then, count the blessing that you have been given by your Creator in heaven, and thank Him for them all day long. This is how you keep your heart free from wounds and turn your tongue into a tree of life!

Those that feel wounded, rejected, shortchanged, or discriminated against in any way must stop cursing and start speaking forgiveness, thankfulness, and blessings!

When we let our hearts fester in bitterness, we develop the habit of cursing and speaking negative words over ourselves and others. But the Scripture teaches in Proverbs 18:21 that life AND death is in the power of our tongues!

We need to use that power in our tongues to speak life INSTEAD of death.

We must Repair the Breach!

If your father on earth was killed or did not live true covenant love with you or your mother (*drama, violence, adultery, unforgiveness, abandonment, separation, or divorce)*, let me introduce you to YAHUAH the Most High, Creator, and **Father of our spirits**.

He can be your FATHER IN HEAVEN if you repent from your sins and believe in His Son Yashua aka Jesus the Savior of Souls!

He will Deliver, Heal, and Restore Your Heart!

Your Father in Heaven **will be there** and **He will care**!

How to Restore Your Heart

Reconnect Your Spirit to Your Father in Heaven:

1. Stop Cursing, Instead Speak Blessings.
2. Give Thanks to God Every day for everything.
3. Forgive others 70x7 (490) times per day, so that God can forgive you from your sins through His Son Jesus. This also means that every time you remember what someone did to you, forgive them again.
4. Develop a life of prayer three time daily and fasting from food for 24 hours weekly. Fasting and prayer are one of the keys to deliverance.

Honor your human Father and Mother:

1. Write out a list of the good character traits and gifts that your parents had.

2. Thank God out loud that you have inherited these gifts and character qualities from your parents every day.

Forgive your human Father and Mother:

1. Write a list of things you forgive your parents for.
2. Write a list of sins that run in your family that you will renounce TODAY.
3. Write a list of good characteristics you are going to replace them with
4. Speak these lists of good things out loud every day

Your Father in Heaven is Ready to Restore Your Heart

Before anything in this earth can be restored, our hearts must be restored first!

Everything we need will start on our inside. Your heart may be broken or it may be wounded. You may know exactly why, or you may not even realize when it happened. But whatever happened, your Father in heaven can heal and restore it!

When you open your heart to your Father in Heaven by speaking to Him and confessing your evil thoughts and words, then committing your mouth to forgiveness and thankfulness, your heart will be on the pathway of healing, deliverance, and hope!

Chapter 2

Father to the Fatherless:
RESTORE YOUR SEXUAL
PURITY and PURPOSE!

A dolescent girls that don't have quality fathers tend to practice riskier sex behaviors than their peers. [1,3] Adolescent boys whose dads fathered them as teenagers are more likely to make babies as teenagers. [4] Quality fathers have a beneficial impact on their children's future sexual health. [2]

The connection between absent fathers and sexual deviations has been very well researched by academia recently. It's also good old-fashioned common sense. A father is the first protector of his children, and a normal father is naturally wired to see, confront, and prevent danger.

Yes, there are some men that are evil or mentally unstable that abuse their own children. Some fathers have minds that are so perverted and twisted away from the purpose of sex, that they will fulfill their extreme lusts on their own children. Those types of fathers should be reported to higher authorities.

Research shows that the majority of fathers are wired to protect their own children. They protect their children by giving them simple wisdom and warning to protect themselves from potential abusers as toddlers. "Don't let anyone touch you in your private parts, and if they do, please tell me."

As their children grow into adolescence, they give them wisdom and instruction according to their beliefs on sexuality.

A healthy father won't just protect his daughters, but also his sons from the harm of sexual abuse and misuse.

"The Talk"

I can remember the time when my father took me into his room for "the talk". I was probably around 11 years old. I can't remember all the details, but I can see it in my mind. I remember seeing in his face and his desire to be clear and sincere with me about this topic.

He explained to me a little bit about what sex was, but the main thing I remember is that he made sure that I knew that the purpose of sex was to have children. This struck me and stuck with me because I had never heard that before. It seems like an obvious point, but it's not often said that the *purpose* of sex is **to have children**.

Our culture of sexual entertainment trains us to think that children are an accidental occurrence if we are not careful during sex. It doesn't teach us that there is an overall purpose for sex other than self-pleasure.

This desire for self-pleasure instead of children is a very slippery slope. How does a man get sexual pleasure without having a child? By sexually abusing an underage girl or boy. If you do get a mature adult pregnant, then she gets an abortion. Logically, the desire for sexual pleasure in selfishness leads to violence.

This is what fathers protect their children from, and this is the sin that our society is filled with. There are so many abandoned, abused, kidnapped, trafficked, and molested children in every nation of the earth.

Am I saying that all sexual sin leads to pedophilia? No. What I am saying is that the logical progression of the unnatural use of sex leads to rape and pedophilia.

What is the Purpose of Sex?

The purpose of a sexual relationship is to turn a man into the ultimate giver. He **gives** his wife pleasure, and he **gives** his wife his sperm as he **gives** her his sexual organ.

After he gives his wife his seed, his wife can produce the fruit of a child. He then gives his wife and children his labor and resources to sustain them. A father is a giver!

Departing from the Natural Use of a Sexual Relationship

> Romans 1: [24] *Therefore God gave them over in the lusts of their own hearts to [sexual] impurity, so that their bodies would be dishonored among them [abandoning them to the degrading power of sin],* [25] *because [by choice] they exchanged the truth of God for a lie, and worshiped and served the creature rather than the Creator, who is blessed forever! Amen.* [26] *For this reason God gave them over to degrading and vile passions; for their women exchanged the natural function for that which is unnatural [a function contrary to nature],* [27] *and in the same way also the men turned away from the natural function of the woman and were consumed with their desire toward one another, men with men committing shameful acts and in return receiving in their own bodies the inevitable and appropriate penalty for their wrongdoing.* [28] *And since they did not see fit to acknowledge God or consider Him worth knowing [as their*

Creator], God gave them over to a depraved mind,
to do things which are improper and repulsive,
[AMPLIFIED BIBLE]

What Were the Romans Doing?

The Roman Empire's culture had a hierarchy of levels of sexual plea-sure based on who was the **giver**, and who was the **receiver**.

It's naturally designed by God that the man is the giver during the sexual act, because his sexual organ is designed to penetrate his wife, who is designed to receive penetration vaginally.

However, the Romanized sinful sex culture had several other options. Anal penetration and oral penetration were the other "acceptable" roles for men in Roman culture. The most demeaning and deroga-tory roles for men were when men became the receivers.[5] Men that received penetration were disrespected and called derogatory names.

The male oral receiver of a female was considered the most base and disrespected man because his mouth was the receiver of the female genitalia. He completely reversed the role and the natural use of a woman to a man. He became a receiver to the woman who was designed to be a receiver, and he was mocked and ridiculed.

So, even in a hyper-sexualized and sinful Roman culture, they real-ized that men are designed to be givers instead of receivers in sexual relationships!

Why? Because even nature teaches us what is right and wrong.

This is why the Scriptures teach that we will be judged from our own words (Luke 19:22), and for violating our own natural consciences (Romans 2:14–15).

One of the takeaways from Romans chapter 1 is that men and women who do these things are degrading themselves even if they don't realize it. When we leave the natural God-given purposes of sex, we degrade ourselves.

Our modern sexual culture is fully Romanized. Even some married couples have created a habit of doing things that are degrading, unfruitful, and reverse natural order… with the same results of disease and degradation in their health and relationship.

In 2014, a team of researchers at the University of Florida found that 11.5% of men and 3.5% of women in the U.S.A were infected with sexually transmitted oral cancer-causing virus HPV. Recently there has been an epidemic of oral cancer even among married men.[6]

What's the solution to this degradation? Submit to God's natural order. Use sex for its natural use. Use sex within a one-flesh marriage covenant and give God the children HE designed to come from your covenant marriage relationship.

Don't take from children; receive children from God and provide for children. Serve your children, love your children, and protect your children from sexual sin.

We Live in A Repackaged Roman Empire Today

Child sex slavery (pederasty) was normal for the Roman Empire, and it can get a stronghold in any culture that starts to reject their conscience and the natural purposes of sex.

When men become sexually selfish and refuse to be givers to their wife and children, it leads our culture down a path of sexual degradation that leads to molestation.

Again, I'm not saying that all sexual sin leads to child sexual abuse. What I am saying is this: the logical progression of the unnatural use of sex leads to rape and molestation.

Once molestation happens, perversion, pedophilia and pederasty can be a continual curse that perpetuates from generation to generation if it is not repented, forgiven, and cleansed.

Hurting people, hurt people. Sexual abuse can incite excessive lust, then fornication, and adultery, then it can descend into homosexuality, child rape, and more perversion in subsequent generations. If the curse is not broken, the cycle continues.

This is partly why in the old covenant, a bastard (illegitimate child) could not even enter into the Congregation of YAH even after 10 Generations (Deuteronomy 23:2)! God did not want unclean sexual desires to get a foothold in His kingdom.

In the old covenant, God wanted to give plenty of time for the curse of fatherlessness to disappear from the family before they could enter into His congregation. That's how important Righteous Family is in the Kingdom of God.

But I have GOOD NEWS for you! With the New Covenant in Christ, you can **break the curse in ONE GENERATION!**

Whenever you repent to the 10 Commandments of God, believe in and follow Jesus the Savior, get baptized in water for a new life, and Become filled with the Holy Spirit, you can be forgiven, made clean, and start a whole new line of righteousness in your family.

No matter the sexual sins in your past or the sexual sins that ran through your family—you can start brand new TODAY.

Even if you were left unprotected by your father and ended up being sexually abused, you can be healed!

Even if your own earthly father was the one who abused you, you have a Father in Heaven that can heal you!

His righteousness is stronger than the sin that was done to you, or the bad example you were shown!

Your <u>purpose is more powerful than your rape or molestation!</u>

Sexual Abuse is Not the End of Your Purpose!

The pain of sexual abuse is deep. It is an atrocity when children are abused by adults or by people who are supposed to protect them, or even by other children as they are left to themselves.

Although the pain is deep and the effects of sexual abuse are strong, God is stronger.

There may have been an unclean spirit (aka demon) that entered in your soul or body through any type of abuse you have suffered. It could have been a cousin, a friend, or someone your parents trusted.

It may not even be physical. It could have been an image, a movie, a joke, or someone showing or telling you how to lust. Mental sexual abuse can be just as damaging to our souls as physical molestation.

Whatever happened, you can ask your Father in Heaven to deliver you from lust, adultery, and perversion.

He will cleanse, heal, and deliver you so that you can obey His commandments; **not to covet what is not yours**, and **not to commit adultery against your marriage covenant**.

You will have a purpose filled life while serving Him!

He will give you a thankful and satisfied soul when you decide to be thankful for what He has given you by honoring your father and mother.

When you honor your father and mother that brought you into the world, God will bless you with what you need to have a successful life. You will not have to covet anything that isn't yours, including sexual things. You will be able to be satisfied with what God has given you in purity.

Just as your father and mother created you through sex, you will use sex not for entertainment or abuse, or merely for self-pleasure. If you have sex, it will be in fruitfulness and productivity in real love.

You can reverse any curse of rape or molestation!

By the power of the Holy Spirit, your sexual purity can be restored!

Restoration of Sexual Purpose

One time a few months ago after he was playing basketball with some older boys, my son mentioned in a dismissive way that "they are all into mating." I guess he heard what the older boys were talking about.

It was funny for him to phrase it that way, but we loved it because of the innocence and insight that it suggests. He was barely 10 years old at the time, but he knew from watching nature videos that mating is for producing offspring. We've also taught him the same thing. So, when he heard the older boys talk about sex, he saw it as them talking about "mating". He knows the purpose of sex, so he was not confused or enticed by other people that talk about it.

It was cute and innocent, but also wise. My wife and I also adopted our son's "mating" terminology when we discuss these things with our children. As adults, we understand that sex is pleasurable, and that God doesn't give you a child every single time you "mate". We also know that knowing the purpose of a thing can help keep us from abusing and misusing the thing.

Purpose produces holiness and Holiness produces purity. In the Kingdom of God there are two ways to live in sexual holiness and purity:

1. Live inside of a marriage covenant and give your body to your spouse.
2. Live outside of a marriage covenant and abstain from sexual activity.

How to Restore Your Sexual Purity and Purpose

1. Write out a list of sexual sins you need to repent from. Then write an explanation of the harm of each and why you will never do them again.
2. Remember the moment you first were sexually abused. It could have been **physical** abuse. It could have been **mental** abuse via a sexually explicit image or song. It could have been a sexually **perverse piece of advice** from a relative or friend. Whatever it was, go back to that moment and give that moment God's response.

   - Reject the sin of that moment.
   - Confess the sin of that moment.
   - Forgive the sin of that moment.
   - Go into that moment and speak the purity and purpose of your life into it.
   - Do this as often as you need to.

3. Pray and ask God to replace your desire for sin with purpose filled holiness and fruitfulness.

4. Confess (speak) these Scriptures on purity and purpose out loud daily:

1 Corinthians 6:[18] Flee fornication. Every sin that a man doeth is without the body; but he that committeth fornication sinneth against his own body. [19] What? know ye not that your body is the temple of the Holy Ghost which is in you, which ye have of God, and ye are not your own? [20] For ye are bought with a price: therefore glorify God in your body, and in your spirit, which are God's.

*Hebrews 13:4 Marriage is honourable in all, and the bed undefiled: but **whoremongers** and **adulterers** God will judge.*

*Job 31: 1 I made a covenant with mine eyes; why then should I **think upon a maid**? [2] For what portion of God is there from above? and what inheritance of the Almighty from on high? [3] Is not **destruction to the wicked**? and a **strange punishment to the workers of iniquity**?*

*1 Thessalonians 4: [2] For ye know what commandments we gave you by the Lord Jesus. [3] For this is the will of God, even your sanctification, that ye **should abstain from fornication**: [4] That every one of you should know how to possess his vessel in sanctification and honour; [5] **Not in the lust of concupiscence, even as the Gentiles which know not God**: [6] That no man go beyond and **defraud his brother** in any matter: because that **the Lord is the avenger of all such**, as we also have forewarned you and testified. [7] For **God hath not called us unto uncleanness, but unto holiness**.*

*Matthew 5:[27] Ye have heard that it was said by them of old time, **Thou shalt not commit***

17

adultery: *28 But I say unto you, That **whosoever looketh on a woman to lust after her hath committed adultery with her already in his heart.** 29 And if thy right eye offend thee, pluck it out, and cast it from thee: for it is profitable for thee that one of thy members should perish, and not that thy whole body should be cast into hell.*

Everything You Lost Can Be Restored by Your Father in Heaven!

If you are willing to forgive those who sinned sexually against you and repent from the sexual sins you've committed against yourself and others, then God can totally restore your sexual purpose and purity.

You must decide to limit all sexual activity within your marriage covenant of your spouse. If you don't have a spouse yet or if you have been separated from your spouse, you must decide not to partake in sexual activities.

There's a much greater purpose for your life than sex. That purpose is to love God and people selflessly, not selfishly. When you find that purpose, you can use sex for God's purpose and restore your sexual purity.

References:

1. Ellis, B.J. Schlomer, G.L. Tilley, E.H. Butler, E.A. (2012). Impact of fathers on risky sexual behavior in daughters: A genetically and environmentally controlled sibling study. Cambridge University Press. https://www.cambridge.org/core/journals/development-and-psychopathology/article/abs/impact-of-fathers-on-risky-sexual-behavior-in-daughters-a-genetically-and-environmentally-controlled-sibling-study/36F38EE0DD D01EEDE65C4F144203359C

2. Kimberly, C. Linton, R.D. (2017). How Time With a Father Relates to Child's Sexual Health, The Family Journal, Volume 25 Issue 2.
https://journals.sagepub.com/doi/10.1177/1066480717699824

3. Ryan, R.M. (2015) Nonresident Fatherhood and Adolescent Sexual Behavior: A Comparison of Siblings Approach. Developmental Psychology, 51(2).
https://content.apa.org/record/2015-02791-002

4. Sipsma, H. Biello, K.B. Cole-Lewis, H. Kershaw, T. (2010). Like Father, Like Son: The Intergenerational Cycle of Adolescent Fatherhood. American Journal of Public Health
https://ajph.aphapublications.org/doi/full/10.2105/AJPH.2009.177600

5. Lamas Jr, M. (2017). The Sin of Cunnilingus, Center for the Study of Christian Origins, University of Edinburgh (New College).
http://www.christianorigins.div.ed.ac.uk/2017/10/25/the-sin-of-cunnilingus/

6. Fox, M. (2017). A Silent Epidemic of Cancer Is Spreading Among Men: Almost every gets this virus and oral sex spreads it. NBC News.
https://www.nbcnews.com/health/health-news/silent-epidemic-cancer-spreading-among-men-n811466

Chapter 3

Father to the Fatherless:
RESTORE HIS HOLY NAME!

J esus saved us way before we knew the original pronunciation of His Name.

His NAME is how you received the Spirit that was then able to further lead you into all Truth.

Jesus came to the Jews that already knew how to pronounce YAHUAH, Yahweh, Yeveh, or Ayahah.

However, He STILL had to introduce them to ABBA Father because they were stubborn, stiff-necked, and rebellious people. They knew how to pronounce His Name but their father was actually the devil; because they obeyed the devil.

ABBA is the most intimate and selective name for YAHUAH.

"ABBA" Father doesn't just mean Daddy.

ABBA means "YES SIR, DADDY."

Ab = Source. Your source is the giver that gives you what you have.

When you call Him ABBA Father, you are saying: "YES SIR, FATHER you are the SOURCE of everything I AM and everything I HAVE, so how could I tell you no?

So, if you can tell Him no—He's not your ABBA yet.

If you can tell Him to wait until later when you are ready—He's not your ABBA yet.

It you can run away from His will when it's not comfortable for you—He's not your ABBA yet.

ABBA, Father is for those that DO what He says WHEN He says it.

> *Mark 14:36 And he said, ABBA, Father,*
> *all things are possible unto thee; take away*
> *this cup from me: nevertheless NOT WHAT*
> *I WILL, but WHAT THOU WILT.*

We all need to get to the point where we are confident enough to OBEY our Father in Heaven's Instructions and call Him ABBA.

JESUS WAS CONFIDENT IN HIS FATHER IN HEAVEN!

Jesus was not the actual physical son of his earthly father, Joseph. It was known in His community that His mother Mary had him before she and Joseph were married.

To a person that didn't believe that He was physically conceived by the Holy Spirit, they would see Jesus as a bastard born from fornication.

Jesus's enemies always found slick ways to remind Him of that in very disrespectful ways. They called him the "son of Mary" instead of Joseph (Mark 6:3). They would cleverly mention "we were not born of fornication," insinuating that Jesus was born of fornication (John 8:41).

Jesus knows what it is like to be looked down upon because your family situation didn't start out as perfect in someone else's eyes.

Yet Jesus was not phased by their sneak disses. Jesus still had total confidence in His relationship with His Father in Heaven! Why? Because He communicated with His Father and did His Father's will.

JESUS DID HIS FATHER'S WILL!

What did Jesus tell His Disciples? "If you have seen ME, you have already seen the Father!" (John 14:9).

When you really see Yahushua (Jesus), it's His character and actions that you see. You see what He has done! He did His Father's will. He honored His Father's name by doing His Father's will. When you see His character—THAT'S WHEN YOU KNOW HIS NAME!

He carried His Father's last name very well! When you see Jesus, then you will also see His Father. When you see His Father, you will figure out how to Honor His Name by refusing to use His Name for vain, selfish, or wicked purposes.

His Spirit will deliver you from Adultery, Lust, Division, Competition, Group-zeal, Hatred, and Drunkenness. God's Holy Spirit can strengthen us so that we no longer have to placate ourselves with sexual sin, excessive consumption, or fights with other groups of people.

The emptiness and the inadequacies and the holes in your heart will be filled up. Your identity will be in your FATHER IN HEAVEN!

You will do powerful works and still be filled with Love, Joy, Peace, Longsuffering, Gentleness, Goodness, Faith, Meekness, and Self-Control.

That's when you will KNOW HIS NAME!

If your father on earth did not give you a last name to be proud of—
Let Me Tell You NOW:

-   No denomination can perfect you.
-   No movement can complete you.
-   No sports team can help you win in real life.
-   Your alma mater cannot lift your spirit or build your soul.
-   No tribe, tongue, nation, or ethnicity can give you a purpose.
-   No gang, political party, club, fraternity, sorority, or secret society can fill the hole in your heart.

All these things are cheap substitutes for the Name of Jesus and His Father in Heaven.

Denominations are incomplete if you are not keeping the Commandments of the Father and His Son.

Spiritual movements may reflect a portion of what God is doing, but they will leave you incomplete if you don't find the whole truth of God.

When your **sports team** wins, your fan life is still the same. When you do what God has commanded you to do, you will win in real life not just fan life!

Your **identity and ethnicity** has a purpose. However, that purpose is not greater than the Great Commandments which are: 1. Loving God with all your heart, soul, mind and strength. 2. Loving your neighbor as yourself.

There are so many **groups of earthly minded people** that try to tempt us to take on an identity that our Creator has not given us. They try to bind our souls to them by convincing us to pledge allegiance, pledge money, or swear oaths.

23

Once our souls are bound, our identities are tied up within that group. Then that group can sway and seduce us into sins against our Father in Heaven's Name.

That's why Jesus instructed us not to swear any oaths:

> Matthew 5: [33] *Again, ye have heard that it hath been said by them of old time, Thou shalt not forswear thyself, but shalt perform unto the Lord thine oaths:* [34] *But **I say unto you, Swear not at all**; neither by heaven; for it is God's throne:* [35] *Nor by the earth; for it is his footstool: neither by Jerusalem; for it is the city of the great King.* [36] *Neither shalt thou swear by thy head, because thou canst not make one hair white or black.* [37] ***But let your communication be, Yea, yea; Nay, nay: for whatsoever is more than these cometh of evil.***

His brother, Apostle James also echoed the same instruction:

> James 5:12 *But above all things, my brethren, **swear not, neither by heaven, neither by the earth, neither by any other oath:** but let your yea be yea; and your nay, nay; lest ye fall into condemnation.*

Swear Definition: Strong's Number 3660; Greek—Omnuo:

1. To swear
2. To affirm, **promise,** threaten, **with an oath**.
3. In swearing, to call a person or thing as witness, to invoke, swear by

Oath Definition: Strong's Number 3727; Greek—Horkos:

1. That which has been **pledged** or promised with an oath.

ELEVATE HIS NAME!

We must demote all these groups that coerce us into pledges and oaths in our hearts. We must renounce them as evil, lest we fall into condemnation. We must choose to elevate the Name of Jesus over them!

You must get to know the Name (Character, Actions, History, and Testimony a.k.a. <u>Commandments) of your Father in Heaven</u>! Once you learn Him, you will fall in love with His Wisdom and His amazing Purpose.

Then you won't feel the pressure in your heart to push any other names. You won't push any other groups, or movements. Your soul will be tied up into His Holy Name.

The true knowledge of His Holy Name will only come from studying, remembering, and rehearsing the Words, Actions, and <u>Commandments of YAHUAH</u> and <u>His Son YAHUSHA</u>!

What's His Name, and What's His Son's Name? Can you tell?

My father always raised us in an atmosphere of following God. We went to several different churches and ministries where I learned the basics of the Scripture and how to sing and worship God.

It wasn't until I was a freshman in college that I started to see that different churches had different beliefs, and that some actually were at enmity with each other.

When I began to learn what denominations were, and why different churches had different "last names," it hurt me to see that the church was divided. I didn't understand why at first. That began my passion for unity in the Body of Christ.

For many of my young adult years, unity was something I thought could happen when denominations put their differences aside and came together to preach the gospel, pray, and worship… then revival would come and unity would happen.

There are many others who think that unity can happen if we can get enough church leaders to have enough good conversations and come to an agreement on religion or politics.

But in reality, the Body will always be Divided and Broken until we stop trying to divide the Father from the Son using the divisions and denominations that came from the ideas of clever men!

Unity can only come from Elohim who Is One! Nothing we can do can bring unity, except repenting and following Him.

Whoever decides to keep the Father's Commandments and the Son's Commandments will be empowered by the Holy Spirit to be One with Elohim.

Whoever decides to break themselves and obey Him will become One in Him and with Him!

The Father and the Son are ONE!

> *Proverbs 30:⁴ Who hath ascended up into heaven, or descended? who hath gathered the wind in his fists? who hath bound the waters in a garment? who hath established all the ends of the earth? what is his name, and what is his son's name, if thou canst tell?*

We need to stop fighting for our brands and groups, and stop contending for our own movements, denominations, ethnicities, and nations. We need to be found laboring for **One Body in Christ** based on the **Truth of the Gospel**, **Scriptural and Historical Accuracy**, and a **Revival and Restoration** of the **Commandments of the Father and the Son**!

The only earthly name we should be fighting for is the name of the **father of our families!**

Whatever your father on earth lacks, you can find it in the name of your Father in heaven!

You won't need the **pride of life** that comes from any title, rank, status, or degree given to you by any fleshly groups of humans.

> *1 John 2:* [16] *For all that is in the world, the lust of the flesh, and the lust of the eyes, and the **pride of life**, is **not of the Father**, but is of the world.*

Once you connect with your Father in Heaven, you will find out that all you need is in His Holy Name!

How to Restore the Understanding of YAHUAH, your Father in Heaven's Holy Name

1. Renounce any pledges or oaths you have made with your mouth to any groups, organizations, or secret societies.
   a. Verbally renounce your pledge in prayer and in writing.
   b. Inform the group that required your pledge that you apologize for any inconvenience, but you have to renounce your pledge in obedience to King Jesus.
2. Renounce any pledges of allegiance you have made to any nations, political movements, or false gods.
   a. Verbally repent for pledging to anything.

    b.   Make a commitment to giving yes or no answers to questions, walking in the integrity of your words.

3.   Repent and ask forgiveness for any support you have given to false denominations, religious groups, or spiritual movements that use the name of Jesus or Yahusha to do their own will instead of keeping His and His Father's Commandments. Communicate with those groups that you will be following the Commandments of Jesus.

4.   Pray for the grace to become satisfied with Honoring His Holy Name in your daily life and obeying His Commandments with others that do the same. Ask God for help and He will give it to you!

5.   Do His will even if it brings pain to your rebellious and your fleshly nature. We all have a sinful nature that we have been taught and fallen into. It will be uncomfortable to replace your will with God's. However, it must be done. You will have more joy in the long run than in the short run.

Your Identity Can be Restored in Your Abba Father's Holy Name

Everyone wants a last name that they can be proud of. Our hearts long for a family name that is respectable and powerful. Many of us lack identity, so we try to find it in gangs; whether they be criminal, political, personal, or spiritual. But the greatest name in Heaven and in earth is the Name of Yahuah Elohim our Creator and His Son Yahusha, our King and Savior.

His family name is not a quarrel or a battle of language, tribe, or ethnicity. His name is based on His character, His history, and His testimony. What has He done? What will He do?

Those that love Him and obey Him are the ones that honor His name.

Definitions come from **The KJV New Testament Greek Lexicon**

Chapter 4

Father to the Fatherless:
RESTORE YOUR
LOGICAL INTEGRITY!

Luke 1:17 And he shall go before him in
the spirit and power of Elias, to turn the
hearts of the fathers to the children, and the
DISOBEDIENT to the WISDOM of the JUST;
to make ready a people prepared for the Lord.

Part of the role of a father is to give you **Logical Integrity**, the type of WISDOM that can ONLY come from OBEDIENCE. Not learning how to obey an earthly father can make it difficult for you to learn how to obey your heavenly Father.

You will not become a child of God if you cannot obey Him. Once you do His Logos (Word), you will build your Logic (thinking abilities).

When Daddy says it, you just do it. You don't debate with Him. You may not understand why He wants you to do something, but if you obey you will figure it out later. Oftentimes, understanding can only come in the process of obedience. The Fear of the LORD is obeying even when you don't understand yet, trusting Yah. That's the fear of YAHUAH. He's Boss!

The Fear of YAH is the BEGINNING of Knowledge (Proverbs 1:7). Intelligence is only properly developed in the structure of doing what is right by the designer and Creator Elohim. Once you learn by experiencing obedience, your brain will put the proper logical connections together. Kinesthetic learning is formed by obedience.

A father's role is to teach us the obedience of respect and action. This creates a higher form of knowledge than simple intellectual intelligence. Learning by doing is the highest form of learning.

In this day of strong delusion and deception, it's <u>not earthly intelligence but INTEGRITY</u> and <u>OBEDIENCE</u> that will save your soul!

The Word of God is the Logos. Our logic should be based on the Logos, and our lives should be built on His Words—plain and simple.

The Scriptures teach that God is actually sending STRONG DELUSION to disobedient people that don't love the truth enough to obey it (2 Thessalonians 2:10–13).

Jesus said if you DO HIS FATHERS WILL, you will know the doctrine (John 7:17). Most of your knowledge of correct Scriptural doctrines will come AFTER you obey it, NOT BEFORE.

WE LIVE IN A GREEK MENTAL CULTURE

Our culture is an extension of the Greek Philosophers… However, we as believers need to <u>switch from a Greek philosopher and debater's mindset</u> to the Mind of Christ—the King of the Jews.

The INTEGRITY of the upright shall guide us (Proverbs 11:3). You will get the knowledge you are looking for ONLY if you have the INTEGRITY to obey.

Unfortunately, due to fatherlessness, abuse, and neglect many of us have open wounds that lead to breaches in our spirit (Proverbs 15:4).

Men are physically designed for strength, protection, and provision. Women are physically designed for beauty, procreation, and helpfulness. There is an order to God's design of the family. Because of God's design, the first and highest authority in a child's life should be their father.

Because of absent fathers, many have not been taught to obey by respect, and to learn knowledge by the experience of obedience. We become overly dependent on egalitarian communication patterns, without the balance of the fear of God and honor for authority. We have been trained to value learning by talking more than we value learning by doing.

In terms of our character, this not only opens us up to devilish influences, but it also leads to breaches in our Logical Integrity—an inability to simply OBEY OUR FATHER'S WISDOM.

In Jeremiah 35, the prophet gives the Word of the Lord to the family of the Rechabites. The Rechabites were a family that obeyed the instruction of their forefather to not drink wine or own any property. There was no logical reason given for the instruction, but they did it anyway.

> *Jeremiah 35: ¹³ Thus saith the LORD of hosts, the*
> *God of Israel; Go and tell the men of Judah and*
> *the inhabitants of Jerusalem, Will ye not receive*
> *instruction to hearken to my words? saith the LORD.*
> *¹⁴ The words of Jonadab the son of Rechab,*
> *that he commanded his sons not to drink wine,*
> *are performed; for unto this day they drink*
> *none, but obey their father's commandment:*
> *notwithstanding I have spoken unto you, rising*
> *early and speaking; but ye hearkened not unto me.*

¹⁵ I have sent also unto you all my servants the prophets, rising up early and sending them, saying, Return ye now every man from his evil way, and amend your doings, and go not after other gods to serve them, and ye shall dwell in the land which I have given to you and to your fathers: but ye have not inclined your ear, nor hearkened unto me.

¹⁶ Because the sons of Jonadab the son of Rechab have performed the commandment of their father, which he commanded them; but this people hath not hearkened unto me:

¹⁷ Therefore thus saith the LORD God of hosts, the God of Israel; Behold, I will bring upon Judah and upon all the inhabitants of Jerusalem all the evil that I have pronounced against them: because I have spoken unto them, but they have not heard; and I have called unto them, but they have not answered.

¹⁸ And Jeremiah said unto the house of the Rechabites, Thus saith the LORD of hosts, the God of Israel; Because ye have obeyed the commandment of Jonadab your father, and kept all his precepts, and done according unto all that he hath commanded you:

¹⁹ Therefore thus saith the LORD of hosts, the God of Israel; Jonadab the son of Rechab shall not want a man to stand before me for ever.

In this account, we see that God respects those that obey their father's instructions, even if their father's instructions weren't HIS specific instructions.

YAH had so much respect for their family that He blessed them and made sure that the Rechabite family would ALWAYS have someone in His presence.

Why does Elohim respect obedience so much? Because He knows that those who can obey their father will be better able to obey Him.

Those that don't obey the Father will never be balanced, consistent, or faithful to WISDOM. They will continue to chase knowledge but remain unstable because of a broken soul. The spirit of confusion comes from a breach in the Spirit that turns into a breach in their logic.

Some lack the integrity to even build their doctrines and beliefs up straight. Our froward (rebellious) hearts cause us to pervert our tongues against His very Commandments!

- Why are we systematically violating **our Father's 10 Commandments** (graven images, idolatry, changing the sabbath, divorce and remarriage adultery, etc.) and thinking it doesn't matter? Especially when Yashua said we won't get to enter heaven without doing His Fathers will (Matt 7:21–24)?
- Why are we **violating His Creation law** if He's the Creator of all wisdom? Do we think we have better ideas about how the world was designed?
- Why do we fall for **deceivers, entertainers, media hypocrites, false apostles, false teachers, Judaizers, crowd chasers, vocabulary word-debaters (subverters), profane Jewish fables, extra-biblical fake books**...when the SCRIPTURES CLEARLY WARN US AGAINST ALL THESE?
- Why do we **buy and sell in the temples (bookstores, merchandise tables in churches)** when Jesus said His Father's house is a house of prayer?
- Why do we continue to **buy and sell discipleship** (classes, conferences, schools) when Jesus did not do it and the Apostles taught against it?

- How do we ignore the Son of God, Yashua's **New Covenant Order, ordinances, and apostolic authority** to try to go back to the Old Covenant Ordinances when Scriptures clearly teach against it (Hebrews 8:13)? Jesus gave new ordinances to His Apostles, yet some choose to follow the feasts of Moses while they ignore Apostolic order.

- How do we still have **denominations and doctrinal divisions** when the Scriptures have been in the common language of the people for almost 500 years now? We can't blame the Dark Ages or the Roman Catholic Church anymore!

These are just a few examples of the ways we are disobedient to the wisdom of our Father in Heaven. The Word of God is the Logos. Our logic should be based on the Logos, and our lives should be built on His Words—plain and simple.

Instead, we lack the Logical Integrity to simply obey God. We get tossed back and forth with strange doctrines from deceivers.

Why are we even open to these deceptions? Is the Pope now our Father? Hebrews claim Abraham as father, but if we rebel against the order of the Son then the devil is our father (John 8:44).

No matter how much knowledge we acquire, or how many teachers, preachers, singers, artists, content creators we heap up to our social media and YouTube accounts: DISOBEDIENCE STILL OPENS US UP TO DECEPTION.

We are tempted to think that our ways are higher than His and our thoughts are higher than His. But they're not (Isaiah 55:9).

We were warned that the last days would be full of silly women carrying layers and layers of sin—ever learning from deceivers but never simply coming to the knowledge of truth by simply repenting, forgiving, and DOING the Word (2 Timothy 3:6).

We must simply obey our Father in Heaven!

Quick Story:

My father helped me out recently. I went over to his house to help him move a freezer. As I left, I mentioned that I ordered a solar panel installation to save on electricity and to avoid power outages which are common in my area. He mentioned that he had planned to do the same thing and he immediately asked me the price of the panels I was purchasing; I told him.

My father called me the next evening. He received three different quotes for solar panels that very day. The company I was buying from was the highest by about $20,000.

He gave me the contacts and suggested I look into getting out of the contract and go with somebody else. A few weeks later, I ended up doing exactly that. My father wanted me to follow a better financial process rather than get duped out of $20,000 by not doing my due diligence!

Even though I'm 40+ years old, my father is still helping me walk in logical integrity! I'm a grown man and I could have been prideful and independent, but I was blessed by simply being obedient to my father's wisdom. He helped me because he cared.

Imagine how much more important it is to be OBEDIENT to WISDOM in spiritual matters!

> *Luke 1:17 And he shall go before him in the*
> *spirit and power of Elias, to turn the hearts of the*
> *fathers to the children, and the DISOBEDIENT*

TO THE WISDOM OF THE JUST; to
make ready a people prepared for the Lord.

Even if you don't have an earthly father, your Heavenly Father will turn your heart back to THE WISDOM OF THE JUST (those that DO HIS WORD and HIS WILL).

He will lead you to good Godly counsel, elders in the Faith, and a new kingdom family of doers of the Word!

How to Restore Your Logical Integrity

1. Think of the last life instruction that you knew in your heart that was right and true but you haven't obeyed it yet. Apologize to God and commit to obeying His Wisdom.
2. What was something your earthly father told you to do that you knew was right but didn't do it? Make a plan and start doing it.
3. Which one of the 10 Commandments do you violate regularly? Make a decision to guard and protect them every day.
4. Find a New Covenant Scriptural teaching that you think sounds extreme and figure out how to obey it. Talk with an Elder or Pastor about your desire to obey more of Jesus's Commandments.
5. Write down 2 or 3 pieces of advice or counsel that you received from someone that you knew in your heart was right—but you didn't like it and made excuses. Make a plan today, and start doing those things without excuse.

You Can Restore Your Mind by Obeying Your Father's Wisdom

There are many that like to talk and debate, but few that like to obey.

Our Father in heaven only gives wisdom to those that are willing to obey. Those that are disobedient will remain ignorant and continue debating and arguing their own vain thoughts and philosophies.

All wisdom comes from our Father in Heaven. When we commit to being HIS children of obedient action, we will learn more and more of His wisdom by experience! We will learn that His Commandments are not grievous and that they are full of His love and care for all.

When we give Him our mind, He will give us the mind of His Son—Jesus Christ His obedient Son.

Chapter 5

Father to the Fatherless:
RESTORE YOUR DISCIPLINE AND PROTECTION!

A fatherless or father-wounded generation finds it difficult to balance freedom with discipline. A good father has compassion and gives generously but is also unmovable on the standards of obedience and discipline in the home that he rules.

If you don't know the love of a father on earth, please receive the love of your Father in Heaven! This part of His love (discipline) won't always feel good, and you won't always be comfortable, but it will make you BETTER!

A father in the home has the ability to break stubbornness and self-will in a child at an early age.

If self-will and stubbornness is not broken at the toddler age, it can destroy the potential of a person's spiritual life AND natural life. When your own will is broken, it's easier to develop self-discipline and self-control.

A will that is broken and bends to authority. It is necessary to get to the next level in our maturity as DISCIPLINED disciples of One Master with One Father in Heaven.

I've told my son several times: There are only a few places that you can learn self-discipline and obedience to authority: home, church, school, sports, work, military, prison, or hell. As you can see, it gets harder and harder the longer you delay learning obedience. Hell is much too late of a place to learn obedience!

In our home, our goal is to train our children to be "voice activated" from when they first learn to understand words. You won't find me or my wife chasing down toddlers in the streets! From when they first learn to understand, they must learn to respond to our voices. My hope is that this will help them learn to respond to their Father in Heaven's voice when they grow up.

Let the Scriptures Determine Your Discipline

Where do we draw the line between discipline and abuse? I believe the Scripture draws those lines.

> *Proverbs 22:15* **Foolishness is bound in the heart of a child**; *but the* **rod of correction** *shall drive it far from him.*
> *Proverbs 23:3* **Withhold not correction** *from the child: for if thou beatest him with* **the rod, he shall not die**.
> *Proverbs 29:15 The* **rod and reproof** *give wisdom: but a child* **left to himself** **bringeth his mother to shame**.

Sometimes it is very tempting for mothers to let children express themselves a little too much. They are in love with the cuteness of their child's personality. If that child is **left to themselves** and not put under discipline, they will bring their mother shame.

I've learned from experience that disobedient actions from children have to be corrected with physical spankings as early as toddler age. As soon as they can understand instructions, they must be held accountable for obeying them.

Good parents also must train their children's tongues. A rebellious and **froward tongue**—that is more prone to express itself than to submit to authority—**will eventually turn the whole body** (James 3:3–6) to rebellious actions and become a major embarrassment.

> *Proverbs 17:20 He that hath a **froward heart** findeth no good: and he that hath a **perverse tongue** falleth into mischief.*

> *Psalms 141:5 Let the **righteous smite me; it shall be a kindness**: and let him reprove me; it shall be an excellent oil, which shall not break my head: for yet my prayer also shall be in their calamities. Psalms 141:5 A **righteous person may strike me** or correct me out of kindness. It is like lotion for my head. My head will not refuse it, because my prayer is directed against evil deeds. [God's Word Translation]*

When my first son was a toddler, I fell victim to the mistake of believing that controlling the verbal expression of a child was going to be harmful for his leadership skills and personality. That was a lie from the pit of hell. Teaching your child that there is a time to obey first and save their own opinions for later will not harm their leadership ability at all. The best leaders are also the best followers. The greatest among us will always be the obedient servant.

When you mold a child's sense of obedience early, it will help them tremendously. Their personality, gift, and calling are given to them by Elohim their Creator and they are unquenchable. The gifts and callings of God are without repentance (Romans 11:29). He doesn't take them back. Those gifts will flourish 10 times brighter after their self-will is broken and reshaped in wisdom and instruction.

When they learn to corral their body and their tongue to the will of their authority that loves them in their home, it will prevent them from having to learn those tough lessons when they fail at school, get fired from a job, join the military, sentenced to prison, or in hell (too late).

Discipline won't squash their potential. Learning how to harness the power of their gifts and personality will take the limits off of their potential!

Scriptures show that the discipline for disobedient action is done by physically spanking with a rod (Proverbs 22:15, Proverbs 23:3, Proverbs 29:15) and discipline of a rebellious tongue is done by smiting the mouth (Psalms 141:5, Proverbs 19:25, John 18:23, Acts 23:2).

This type of biblical discipline should be gentle and limited. It should be based on logic, not on emotion, fits of rage, or screaming and yelling. The purpose of discipline is to train a child how they should live, speak, and work—not to get revenge or express our anger at them.

I believe it's better to discipline on a time delay than to discipline in fits of emotional anger. Children learn by example, and if you can't control your emotions or your tongue, you cannot expect a child to control theirs. If you feel overwhelmed with anger, always wait until later.

My wife and I also have a rule that we will only spank a child according to the number of their age. If they are five years old, they get five swats for disobedience.

The plan is that as they get older, we won't have to spank them at all. Nobody wants to receive or even give 10, 11, 12, 13, 14 spankings.

As they say: "Ain't nobody got time for that." The earlier you start with healthy discipline; the easier life is for everyone.

Discipline comes from love; it is not abuse. Abuse comes from fear. Abuse comes from substance abuse, and alcoholism. Abuse comes from lack of understanding of the Commandments and the Love of God. Abuse comes from selfishness. A loving father that keeps God's Commandments should never fear that his discipline will be received as abuse.

I caught my mistake early, but it's an ongoing battle to develop the training and self-control that I could have given my son when he was two years old. The longer you delay it, the more work it takes.

We also have several other forms of positive and negative training and discipline with our children such as: chores, extra chores, allowance, losing allowance, fake money, a treat store, politeness standards, pushups, etc. We are not perfect. We are learning as we go and we have made many mistakes but everything we do; we try to do it in love.

Discipline is Love

Discipline is a form of love. A commitment to both giving healthy discipline and boundaries is one of the highest forms of love we can give.

Fathers are instructed in Scripture not to make their children angry on purpose, but to make them mature and grow them up by feeding and caring for them and warning them to obey the instructions of God.

> *Ephesians 6:4 And, ye fathers, provoke not*
> *your children to wrath: but bring them up in*
> *the nurture and admonition of the Lord.*

Godly discipline breaks the rebellion and self-will of sin, but it also strengthens their faith in the rewards for obedience at the same time. A father's goal in discipline is to strengthen them in their hearts, not break their courage.

> *Colossians 3:21 Fathers, provoke not your*
> *children to anger, lest they be discouraged.*

Each child must be built up in their **confidence that there is a reward** for self-discipline. **Keep a positive spin on your disciplinary actions so that your child doesn't lose hope!** This is a very important part of a father's relationship with his child.

Sometimes Abuse Does Happen

There are some that have suffered abuse from mentally unstable fathers or mentally unstable mothers that lacked the support they needed from their husbands.

We have to be careful not to let our experiences with abuse turn our hearts against healthy discipline and authority.

When people have abuse in their family, it colors their perception towards family authority.

When people experience church abuse, they get suspicious towards any form of spiritual authority.

Unfortunately, some of us have been abused by authority to the point where we see **even Godly healthy authority** as a threat to our freedom.

Don't flee from the lies of abuse and oppression to run to the lies of lawlessness and disorder.

For example, you may have grown up in a home where you were disciplined emotionally instead of logically and it degenerated into abuse.

When it's time for you to discipline your children, you may not want to do it at all because you have associated discipline with abuse. Instead of choosing the balanced godly discipline, you may choose no discipline at all, and end up with a child that brings you shame, or ruins their own life with sin.

The Discipline that Starts with a Father is Needed in Other Areas of Life

There are other areas where discipline and authority are necessary. There are also different rules of engagement for all forms of authority. The father has a certain role of authority in the home. As husband, he is in a place of authority over his wife, though he doesn't treat her like a child, but like a friend and partner-in-life.

The government has authority over punishing criminals and collecting taxes, but they don't have any authority over the bodies, minds, and souls of our families.

The congregational ministry has spiritual authority to teach, preach, and persuade people to obey God's commandments, but it cannot command a family or manipulate them in their personal affairs. The only disciplines that a Pastoral ministry can give is public rebuke, and the forbidding of fellowship (1 Timothy 5:20, 1 Corinthians 5:9–13).

All in all, we need to have a healthy view of balanced authority in all areas. Our respect for the protection and discipline of authority should start as a healthy child/father relationship, then spread out in a healthy way to all the areas of our lives.

ORDER IN THE MARRIAGE AND FAMILY:

Word to my sisters: your gift, talent, or intelligence does not make you the head of your home. A wife can have the skillset for a six-figure job and she should use those skills if needed, but she will never be a husband or father. In **the structure of the family,** her role is to help her husband, nurture her children, and manage her household. Subtle or aggressive tactics to lead your husband will bring confusion and disorder into your house. If you see something he does not see, pray for him, and communicate with respect and deference. God is honored when we follow HIS ordained order.

Even in the home, it's not always easy to follow an imperfect leader. Every husband has that first bad decision that shifts their marriage from the "honeymoon phase" to the "my wife won't trust me anymore, so she talks to me like her son" phase.

I remember one of my first leadership mistakes as a young husband. My wife asked me to use my truck to transport some furniture. I think it may have been a bed frame. She wanted me to secure it and tie it down with some ties. I didn't have any ties and didn't think I needed them. So, I just decided to go without tying it down. Needless to say, it fell out of the truck and broke into pieces on the way to my destination. When you make that first mistake, it can break your confidence as a leader.

When you make that first mistake, it can cause your wife to lose her confidence in your leadership.

In reality, the husband is responsible for his mistakes and he is **still the leader** regardless if he makes mistakes or not. God will punish the leader for his mistakes, will pay for the mistakes of a leader, and will keep His order in place to bless the whole family. God is the Leader of Leaders. He is higher than all.

Whatever the cost was for that broken bed frame, it's absolutely nothing compared to how Yah can reward a house that flows in His designated peace and order. We have to have a higher vision of what God can do than the mistakes we can make.

If a wife tries to usurp authority or punish her husband for his mistakes, she is usurping the authority of God and she will be punished the same as her husband. It's better to pray to God, submit to the chain of command, and trust the Most High to bring forgiveness and restoration for all mistakes.

There are many situations where husbands make mistakes that are more evil than breaking furniture. There are other situations where the wife treats her husband with contempt and makes him feel less than a man. Bitterness can turn a sweet relationship into a sour one. But a healthy marriage is going to be full of forgiveness both ways. Two imperfect people can maintain a friendship where they can each fulfill their role, keep their covenant, and the Father above will give them grace to make life enjoyable and rewarding!

It's better to have a household of order than one of disorder. There is a healthy way for a submissive wife to communicate concerns while also giving her husband confidence to make the right decision. A wise woman also will trust in God that He will take care of the whole family and have everyone's back whether mistakes are made or not.

Letting your husband lead without resistance will grow his confidence and turn him into a better leader, a better husband, and a better father.

Order is based on position, not on intelligence. You may be smarter than your boss at work, but you still follow their instruction because of their position.

The Scriptures always give instructions in the right order. If you look at Ephesians 5 and Colossians 3, you'll see the order of obedience:

> Wives obey husbands, then husbands love wives without bitterness.
> Children obey parents, then fathers don't provoke wrath in your children.
> Employees obey bosses, then bosses pay fair and treat employees equally.

The Scripture never demonstrates a wise woman submitting to their husbands **only** if their husbands are great leaders. The Scriptures demonstrate that wise women obey their husbands and help them learn to lead by being submissive (easy to lead), allowing themselves to be led and praying for them along the way. Foolish husbands are punished by God, not by their wives.

Abigail tried her best to submit and help her husband even though he was a bona fide fool. God rewarded her when Nabal got killed and made her the wife to King David (See 1 Samuel 25).

Sara followed Abraham even when he was making leadership mistakes. And eventually he became the father of faith, and she was rewarded greatly.

A wise woman will submit to her husband's leadership development in every area **except** anything that violates the 10 Commandments of the Father in Heaven. She will pray, obey, and support her covenant husband until he becomes the king God made him to be. Then they will inherit the grace of life together.

ORDER IN THE MINISTRY AND CONGREGATION:

Immature prophetic gifts are often tempted to try to direct and influence congregations with their gifts of revelation without first serving and submitting to God's order. The Family of God is not designed to be directed by gifts and talents, but by the character of those that operate in humility, service, integrity, and faithfulness. Biblically qualified elders prove their character with sound doctrine and integrity. I love the gifts of prophecy, tongues, and interpretation, but we have to learn how to love with decency and order as well.

God has given gifts to everyone and he doesn't take them back. However, character is not given to anyone. Character is developed by obedience, submission, service, and faithfulness. That's how we bear the best fruit possible.

Those with revelation and special gifts must submit their gift to prayer, faithful service, and demonstration of a life of humility and integrity. There are too many gifted people with messed up lives, messed up marriages, and messed up families. Fruitlessness and destruction come when we don't follow God's ordained order.

Rebellion always seems like freedom until our REAL enemy shows up! Godly authority is not our enemy. Satan is our real enemy. It seems fun to have independence and freedom from spiritual authority, but fake freedom becomes bondage again very quickly.

Eve thought she was getting wisdom, freedom, and enlightenment when she listened to the serpent and got out of order with her husband. It didn't turn out well for anyone.

A spirit of rebellion is Satan's domain. It leaves us open to being deceived by false doctrines, and it steals our spiritual inheritance from us, our children, and our disciples. This is why the Scriptures call it "unprofitable for you."

> *Hebrews 13: [17] Obey [listen to] them that have the rule over you, and submit yourselves: for they watch for your souls, as they that must give account, that they may do it with joy, and not with grief: for that is <u>unprofitable for you</u>.*

Refusing to submit yourself and listen to qualified spiritual authorities can create losses in our life that we will never even see or understand.

God can <u>protect you when you submit</u> to His Order. He is our Father in Heaven, and our fathers on earth were meant to reflect His protection, compassion, and discipline for us.

Temper Tantrums Cannot Help Us Avoid Repentance

Unfortunately, whenever God sends messengers to bring back His message of returning to His Commandments and His Order, one of the most common responses is a spiritual temper tantrum.

If you've ever raised a toddler into a child, you know the stages of emotional manipulation that comes when their will is being conformed into obedience:

- silence or denial "huh?" not acknowledging the instruction
- temper tantrums
- blame-shifting, responsibility avoidance
- negotiation "if I do this, then you gotta…"
- "you don't love me"
- self-hatred, "woe is me"

This is the same thing we are tempted to do spiritually, when our Father in Heaven commands us to repent, mature, and grow up.

Toddlers are so cute. They are so expressive and talented. If you're honest you don't even really want to discipline them. You enjoy them too much! They get a lot of sympathy for their rebellion, just like my first son when we were ignorant first-time parents.

But guess what? Silence, denial, emotional manipulation, negation, and blame shifting won't work with God. He's not an ignorant first-time parent. He is a Father to the fatherless. He's been doing this a long time and He knows EXACTLY what He's doing to make us better.

He IS patient, and He IS kind, and His mercy IS brand new every morning… BUT HE STILL COMMANDS US TO REPENT. We must learn to calm down, repent, and keep His Commandments.

Our ABBA Father loves us, but He ignores our spiritual temper tantrums. He only responds to faith and obedience.

> *Acts 17:30 And the times of this ignorance*
> *God winked at;* ***but now commandeth***
> ***all men every where to repent****:*

Our Heavenly Father's Commandments are GOOD for us!

He's a Good, Good Father! His Commandments are Not Grievous. They are for our PROTECTION.

> *1 John 5:3 For this is the love of God,*
> *that we keep his commandments: and*
> *his commandments are not grievous.*
> *Grievous-Greek: Barus—Definition:*
> *1. heavy in weight*
> *2. burdensome, severe, stern, weighty, of*
> *great moment, violent, cruel, unsparing*

- Anyone that tells you that God's Commandments are too heavy is a LIAR. His yoke is easy, and His burden is light.
- Anyone that tells you that God's Commandments are hard to carry is a LIAR. His Commandments are simple to pick up and adapt into your lifestyle. The only thing you lose is sin.
- Anyone that tells you that God's Commandments are extreme and severe is a LIAR. His Commandments make perfect sense, and they are useful for life and love.

- Anyone that tells you that God's Commandments are stern and mean is a LIAR. His Commandments are gentle, and they are effective in producing good results for everyone involved.
- Anyone that tells you that God's Commandments are unwieldy and inconvenient to life is a LIAR. His Commandments are only inconvenient to our INIQUITY, PRIDE, VANITY and STUBBORNESS. They are good for life, love, and fruitfulness. The humble will hear and be GLAD!
- Anyone that tells you that God's Commandments are violent is a LIAR. God has hated violence from the beginning, His Commandments bring peace and order.
- Anyone that tells you that God's Commandments are cruel is a LIAR. God's Commandments expose our cruel and insidious hidden evils to make room for peace and blessings.
- Anyone that tells you that God's Commandments are unsparing is a LIAR. God has mercy brand new every morning for those that repent from sin and cherish His Commandments.

HIS Holy Habitation is the Place of His Order

God's Commandments are His testimony, and they create the atmosphere of HIS holy habitation which are love and protection for the weak.

> *Psalms 68:5 A father of the fatherless, and a judge of the widows, is God IN HIS holy habitation.*

- God uses good fathers and husbands to protect women and children from abusers and predators.
- God uses caring fathers and brothers to protect women from abusive men or husbands.

- God uses good shepherds (elders) and overseers to protect His people against spiritual wolves, false apostles, and abusive pastors.
- God uses righteous preachers to protect the weak against abusive leadership by preaching the gospel, preaching God's judgement, and teaching the 10 Commandments.
- God uses governments to protect citizens against criminals and domestic abusers.
- God sends bigger governments to bring down oppressive governments.

God cares for everyone! However, we cannot live in rebellion against the authorities that God Himself has sent to protect us, and then complain to God about not protecting us. The rebellious will dwell in a dry land.

Psalms 68:6 God setteth the solitary in FAMILIES: he bringeth OUT those which are BOUND with chains: but the REBELLIOUS dwell in a dry land.

Patriarchy Works.

The vast majority of Fathers PROTECT their daughters, and don't MOLEST their daughters. For those that do: the Police and the Preacher get involved. The government bears the sword to punish evildoers.

The preacher bears the sword of the Word of God to bring conviction and repentance.

But unfortunately, this world loves DISORDER so much that it sees ORDER as a Dangerous Problem: we have a whole culture of feminism that rebels against patriarchy and the role of men in the home.

Then this same anti-patriarchy culture cries & complains about the Results of DISORDER: children growing up with no direction and no discipline, abusing themselves with drugs and alcohol, abusing each other sexually, and committing murder on the babies.

Rebellion Fails. The rebellious will dwell in a dry land (Psalms 68:6).

Protection comes from Protectors. This is the ONLY solution!

The TEN Commandments (Law of Liberty) WORKS. It is in perfect alignment with the Spirit of the LORD! Where the Spirit of the Lord is, there is Liberty (2 Corinthians 3:17).

The Father and the Son are One. The Son of God (Christ) doesn't rebel against His Father's House Rules.

When a society doesn't have the 10 Commandments as a foundation, **the fear of God is not in the atmosphere**. This creates more opportunities for abuse from fathers, pastors, employers, and governments.

Where there is no fear of God, governments are more likely to enforce caste-system style policies that give economic strength to preferred groups and races, and kill or create slaves and prisoners out of people groups that are despised.

Where there is no fear of God, employers are more likely to abuse employees by trying to squeeze every drop of profit from them instead of helping them make a long-term profit from their labor.

Where there is no fear of God, pastors are more likely to sexually or financially abuse people that follow them for their spiritual gifts, instead of teaching and serving them and operating with integrity to the Scriptures.

Where there is no fear of God, fathers are more likely to be violent towards their wives and children, or waste their resources on alcohol, sexual sin, or gambling.

You may have been <u>hurt and abused</u> in your past, but in order for true healing and deliverance to manifest in your life you will need to forgive, be healed, and rebuild your TRUST in the protection of your Father in Heaven. His protection is found in these institutions:

1. His TEN COMMANDMENTS
2. Christ's New Covenant Authority in the Gospel
3. Manhood and Fatherhood—Family Leadership.
4. Women and Children being cared for and protected under authority.
   (See 1 Corinthians 11:3).

He is a FATHER TO THE FATHERLESS, and a DEFENDER OF WIDOWS.

BUT HE CAN ONLY FULLY DEFEND THOSE THAT ARE FULLY OBEDIENT TO HIM.

The Faith and Authority Connection in Scriptural History

Yahushua taught us that Gentiles (Romans/Europeans) had more faith than Israelites (Ewes/Bantus/Negroes) because they are more comfortable with authority. He was amazed and openly marveled at the faith of a Roman centurion who was a strong supporter of the Jews

> *Luke 7: ⁶ Then Jesus went with them. And when*
> *he was now not far from the house, the centurion*
> *sent friends to him, saying unto him, Lord, trouble*
> *not thyself: for I am not worthy that thou shouldest*
> *enter under my roof:⁷ Wherefore neither thought*
> *I myself worthy to come unto thee: but say in a*

*word, and my servant shall be healed. ⁸ For I also
am a man SET UNDER AUTHORITY, having
UNDER ME SOLDIERS, and I say unto one,
Go, and he goeth; and to another, Come, and he
cometh; and to my servant, Do this, and he doeth
it. ⁹ When Jesus heard these things, he marvelled
at him, and turned him about, and said unto the
people that followed him, I say unto you, I have
NOT SO GREAT FAITH no, NOT IN ISRAEL.*

Jesus could not find the same level of faith that was in this Roman centurion anywhere in Israel. Generations of oppression and trauma from several captivities turned the Israelites into a perverse people that became comfortable with rebellion than with the new order and authority that Christ had with Moses.

The Israelites thought they were submitting to the Father by obeying Moses, but they rejected His Son, the prophets and apostles He sent. They thought they were keeping the Torah by following the Old Covenant order, but were blind to the prophecy in Isaiah 8:16 that foreshadowed the authority of Torah being transferred to the New Covenant Disciples.

Those Jews that resisted kingdom authority were punished. Women became our rulers and children became our oppressors, as was prophesied in Isaiah 3:12. Meanwhile, the gospel of Christ's authority flourished in Gentile nations—just as the Messiah had told His disciples previously.

The New Covenant grew powerful in Gentile nations, that it had to be corrupted and turned into idolatry by the Roman Empire. Although. the Roman Empire murdered disciples by the thousands, it couldn't stop people from following Jesus. Therefore, they had to DECEIVE the followers of Jesus to start breaking the 10 Commandments of the Father! The Roman Emperor Constantine created the false Roman

Catholic church as a government-ruled substitute for the Body of Christ.

Returning to the Authority of the Father and the Son and the Man and the Woman

Before it was corrupted by politics, the power of faith in Jesus did great things among Gentiles all over the world. Even to this day, the power of your faith remains connected to your understanding of authority. Demons in the unseen realm will follow spiritual protocols even when we can't see them.

The Roman Centurion understood spiritual authority by understanding natural authority and was able to manifest great faith for uncommon miracles. When we follow the chain of command in our families and congregations, we will see the glory of God manifest on a greater level.

> *1 Corinthians 11: 1 Be ye FOLLOWERS OF ME, even as I ALSO AM OF CHRIST. ² Now I praise you, brethren, that ye remember me in all things, and KEEP THE ORDINANCES, as I delivered them to you. ³ But I would have you know, that the HEAD of every MAN is CHRIST; and the head of the WOMAN is the MAN; and the HEAD of CHRIST is GOD.*

We will see the glory of God return to the Body of Messiah when women submit to men, and men submit to Christ's authority, who is already completely submitted to the commandment of His Father YAHUAH.

That's when we will see an outbreak of healing, deliverance, reconciliation, and the restoration of all things in our generation!

As we connect in the authority of the family of God, the power of faith will flow and the gospel of the Kingdom will flourish again for both the Jew and the Gentile in One Body!

Hebrews 13:17 OBEY THEM THAT HAVE THE RULE OVER YOU, and SUBMIT YOURSELVES: for they WATCH FOR YOUR SOULS, as they that must give account, that they may do it with joy, and not with grief: for THAT IS UNPROFITABLE FOR YOU.

How to Restore Your Discipline and Protection

1. Repent for any rebellion you have against the Father's 10 Commandments. Study them more and learn them. Realize that His Commandments are not grievous, they are love and for our discipline and protection.
2. Repent for any rebellion or disobedient attitudes that you had or still have against your father on earth.
3. Wives: Repent for any time you attempted to usurp the authority of your husband or refused to obey him and see him as the ruler and protector of your physical life.
4. Pray for healing from fatherlessness, neglect, or abuse you may have suffered from your father.
5. Pray for healing from "church hurt" if you were sexually abused, financially abused, or taught lies against the Scripture.
6. Find a congregation that values the Father's 10 Commandments over political power and values the New Covenant Order of Jesus and His Apostles over the ceremonial laws of Moses.
7. Submit yourself to a healthy Commandment-keeping, New Covenant Congregation. Help them build up disciples, pray night and day, and preach the gospel to the community.

**Your Discipline and Protection Will Be
Restored by Your Abba Father!**

A healthy relationship with discipline and authority is something that a child should receive from their father early in life. A lack of a father in the home, or an abusive father in the home can ruin that experience for a child.

However, it is never too late to learn submission and obedience to your Father in Heaven. You can study His Commandments, learn His wisdom, follow His Son, be filled with his Spirit, join His Congregation, and become a Disciple of Jesus.

Discipline in every area of your life will lead to greater effectiveness in every area of your life, and you will see God's power show up for you and yours!

Chapter 6

Father to the Fatherless:
RESTORE YOUR
KINGDOM FAMILY!

Many people have suffered from abuse and false doctrine from so-called "spiritual fathers." This is not a biblical concept.

In Matthew 23:9, Jesus instructed us to "call no man on earth your father, for One is your Father, even your Father in Heaven."

It's perfectly normal to have a good and affectionate relationship with an elder or pastor, especially if they were instrumental in preaching salvation. If you were raised without a father like apostle Timothy in Scripture, you may have a fatherly relationship with someone who disciples you in the faith such as apostle Paul.

However, when "spiritual fatherhood" is used to manipulate and transgress the boundaries that Jesus has set for His Body, this can cause great harm to the saints of God.

The Most High has used me to heal, mend, deliver, and set free a number of people that have experienced "church hurt." Church hurt happens when hurting people, hurt people. It also happens when unqualified spiritual wolves see the sheep as their personal meal instead of as the Lord's flock.

> *Matthew 18:6 But whoso shall offend **one** of these **little ones** which **believe** in me, it were better for him **that** a millstone were hanged about his neck, and **that** he were drowned in the depth of the sea. 7 Woe unto the world because of **offences**! for it **must** needs be that **offences come**; but woe to that man by whom the **offence cometh!***

Art Imitates Life

It's amazing to see that the root of some of the evilest people in the world is "church hurt" and abuse from men who were unqualified to be spiritual leaders in the Body of Christ. I'm sure you've heard of someone that was sexually or financially abused by a preacher, priest, or a congregation then totally turned against God. Some of the biggest Satanist rock stars, vilest rappers, and devout atheists were abused by a false spiritual authority early in their life.

You don't have to look too far to find this testimony. You can study famous artists and their personal testimonies. Most started out in church and had a bad experience.

You can see church hurt in the news reports of Catholic priests abusing young boys. It's affected many cultures.

I can remember in high school, "religious hypocrisy" was the consistent theme in every single book assigned by one of my English teachers. It seemed like every story we read had someone that was abused by the church before turning to a life of self-expression and following their own sinful way. Religious hypocrisy is a very consistent them in the art that imitates life.

It's often used as a very convenient excuse. But is this really an excuse for sinners, unbelievers, and blasphemers? Absolutely NOT!

Everyone is accountable for their own actions. People must humble themselves to be healed, delivered, learn how to forgive, and learn how to obey God instead of violating their own conscience. Someone "in church" doing you wrong is never an excuse for you to do wrong, when you have your own conscience that tells you right and wrong.

We Need to Make it Right

People who have "church hurt" need to be accountable to God for their own conscience. They must forgive the ones who hurt them, if they want to be forgiven of their sins. But people that have been "church hurt" also need to see a REAL representation of Jesus. Real SERVANTS, serving the real BODY of CHRIST, following the Word of God and not following traditions of men.

We must be passionate about bringing HEALING as well as bringing SOLUTIONS!

Nothing that I say or do is meant to trivialize the attacks of a **wolf-pack** on one of God's precious lambs. There are packs of spiritual wolves and adulterers who prey on God's people for their own gain. They teach lies, live lies, and market themselves as preachers and pastors. This is wrong and will be punished severely.

However, I speak in a spirit of healing, correction, and repentance when I say that not all "church hurt" is bad.

Sometimes, **the Good Shepherd can hurt you too**, with His Shepherd's rod getting you back into the flock with a sharp word (Ecclesiastes 12:11).

Sometimes sheep go astray, and God sends the Word through His leaders to get them back in line with God's flock. This **hurts our pride,** but it is helpful for our souls.

JESUS is the Shepherd in charge of disciplining **His Sheep**.

Sometimes **the Surgeon of our Souls can cut you**; but the Surgeon's sharp tool is cutting something harmful out of you, or fixing something that is out of order, and setting it in its right place.

Surgical operations can be painful and can cause soreness, but God also gives His love as an anesthesia when we worship Him in Spirit and in Truth.

JESUS is the Surgeon that will not tolerate cancerous growths that will eventually destroy **His Body**.

There are 3 DIFFERENT types of Church hurt:

- The **Wolf** hurts you for his <u>own</u> **<u>gain</u>**.
- The **Shepherd** hurts you to get you <u>back into</u> **<u>righteousness</u> <u>and</u> <u>Godly fellowship</u>**.
- The **Surgeon** hurts you to <u>cut a</u> **<u>harmful cancer</u>** out of the body, or repair and reset something broken in you.

Not all church hurt is bad.

BE WISE ENOUGH to discern between the good hurt and the bad hurt!

No matter what you've suffered, YAH will always lead you to good Godly counsel, elders in the faith, and a new kingdom family of doers of the Word!

He will lead you to faithfulness and accountability, making disciples and co-laboring in the gospel with a team of believers in New Covenant Order.

Your Father in Heaven will Give You a New Kingdom FAMILY: An ECCLESIA/CONGREGATION/ASSEMBLY with ORDER, STRUCTURE, INTEGRITY, and ACCOUNTABILITY.

When you had a father that is not abusive but compassionate, you have learned a healthy attitude towards correction. You realize that correction is for your own good. You may even get to the point where you <u>ask for and desire correction as a form of help</u> for you to accomplish God's will in your life.

If you've never been corrected due to an abusive or absent father, you might tend to fall into an unhealthy attitude towards order and structure. When you are raised in a dysfunctional family where the father doesn't seek God and the mother is rebellious or on her own, it has the potential to change how comfortable you are with family structure.

This is no excuse! Even without a good father, there are many ways that God can teach us to be submissive to correction. Grandparents, uncles, aunts, pastors, teachers, coaches; there are many people in our lives that give us structure and correction. How we respond is up to us. Our Father in Heaven can give us whatever we lack!

We have to take account of ourselves. Are we comfortable with disorder or order? Are we comfortable with authority, or do we prefer to usurp and ignore authority?

Do we realize that we are instrumental to something greater than us, or are we more comfortable with dysfunction and individual thinking?

**There is a Structure in God's Assembly
that is Necessary for Love to Flow**

Order and structure feels like abuse and manipulation to those who never had them in a healthy, loving, and fruitful manner, but it's actually critical for the flow of Love.

There are a few concepts we must understand regarding the Order of God's Family:

Rebellion and Independence is not freedom, it's bondage. Wise Boundaries and Logical Integrity (building up your thoughts on obeying what God says) <u>create true Freedom.</u>

- Wise boundaries, limits, and discretion don't restrict your freedom, they actually create and empower your freedom aka free dominion. Because if you can do anything you want, you can't get anything all the way done.
- When we are not comfortable with Godly authority, healthy accountability, and structural order;—we need to check our character and our heart. **Ask God to mend your heart and restore what's missing**.
- **The worst lies that we can tell are the ones we tell our own selves**. If we love to see and hear religious entertainment but we aren't doing the Word of God—we are our own biggest deceivers (James 1:22).
- If you are seeking after more knowledge, but not seeking after OBEYING what you already know—check your soul. **Something more important than knowledge is missing from your heart**.
- **A lack of integrity leads us right into deception and strong delusion** when we are "ever learning, but never coming into the knowledge of the truth."
- **Love can flow most powerfully when the Family is connected** in fellowship, and every member is functioning in their proper role (1 John 1:7, Ephesians 4:15–16).

We may need **healing**. We may need **deliverance**. Our Father in heaven can freely give us both and connect us into His Family of Love.

Even Father Abraham's Family had Drama

Abraham was a friend of God, and the father of faith, who was honored by Elohim for teaching his employees and servants to obey the commandments of God. But Abraham was far from perfect. Abraham had a couple of character flaws that came from the iniquities of fear and doubt.

He was a mighty warrior who fought and won great battles (Genesis 14), but other times his fear caused him to put his wife in danger when he thought other kings were going to kill him for his wife (Genesis 12, 20).

Abraham's first son Ishmael was born to Abraham in a time when Abraham was faithless, disobedient, and living in disorder and sin from unbelief.

God had promised Abraham a son. Instead of waiting for God to give Him the Promised child, Abraham listened to his wife's false counsel and made Ishmael through Hagar, one of his servants. Hagar was a servant that they had gotten from Egypt.

It was customary in ancient Eastern cultures to have children through servants of the wife in order to grow the family. However, that was against God's natural law and order for the design of marriage, and the adverse results show up every time men took multiple women as sexual partners. God was so annoyed with what Abraham did, that He didn't speak to him again for 13 years!

Abrahamic DRAMA: Sarah the Wife vs Hagar the Servant

In Genesis 16, we see that Hagar became a bit arrogant when she had Abraham's baby and started acting out a bit. Envy and pride, mixed with birthing and nursing hormones has the potential to bring a lot of harm to any relationship. Ask any mother throughout history how that can work!

At the end of the day, Hagar didn't ask to be Abraham's second wife; it was Sarah's idea. But Hagar was the one that got disciplined harshly, and ended up running away from her family, into the desert.

Hagar ended up alone in the desert pregnant with Abraham's child. What would happen to Hagar? Would her child be fatherless?

In the end, YAH stepped in. He saw her situation and helped her. He sent an angel to check on her, told her to return to Sarah, and submit to the one who did wrong to her. Then the angel blessed Hagar and named her son Ishmael, "because YAHUAH has HEARD her affliction."

Her Father in Heaven Heard her!

After this situation, Hagar knew God on a much deeper level. She became the only person in the Scripture who gave Elohim a name. Everyone else in the Bible was given a name by Elohim. Hagar was the only one who gave Elohim a Name! What was the name she gave the Most High?

El Roi: "El Sees"

> Genesis 16:^{13} And she called the name
> of the LORD that spake unto her, Thou
> God seest me: for she said, Have I also
> here looked after him that seeth me?

Her Father in Heaven Saw Her!

YAH saw Hagar, heard Hagar, and cared about Hagar.

God saw her situation, and helped her, and gave her and her son a blessing. In the end, she was instructed to submit herself back under her leader and reconnect to her family.

Hagar had to stop acting in pride and rebellion. She had to forgive and submit to the person who made a mistake and did her wrong. Hagar was also greatly rewarded and developed a much higher level of closeness with her Father in heaven.

After all Hagar suffered, she still was instructed to return and submit to her leader. In some family or employee situations, the Most High will have you submit to a leader who makes mistakes, because He is going to bless you regardless of their mistakes.

No, you do NOT have to submit to spiritual leaders that continually listen to lies or consistently violate the Commandments of God, but in most relationships there should be mercy and submission one to another even through mistakes and miscommunications. If you work things out through the ups and downs, God will be able to bless everyone that much more!

What can we learn from Hagar and Sarah?

- If you were done wrong by someone in authority over you, your heavenly Father sees, and hears, and cares.
- If you have done wrong to someone in authority over you, God still has a blessing for you.
- God develops a great intimacy and closeness to those who suffer unjustly.
- Just because you were done wrong doesn't mean you can live a life of total rebellion.
- If you submit yourself to God's commandment, and do right by Him, He will make sure that you are blessed, rewarded, vindicated, and supported.
- God wants you to be in His Family of faith.

Ishmael: the Mistake Child Loved by His Father in Heaven

Ishmael didn't ask to be born in a bad situation. He didn't ask to be born to the second wife. But Ishmael came into the family through impurity, and he developed impure character.

Ishmael was 14 years older than Isaac, Sarah's son. Ishmael knew that Isaac was the promised, covenant, miracle child; the one that would inherit his father Abraham's riches, wealth, land, property, assets, and servants. That could create some envy and jealousy in a teenager.

When Ishmael responded to Isaac's weaning celebration by mocking Isaac, Sarah got angry and asked Abraham to put Ishmael and his mother out of the house. Sound familiar?

Sarah started the drama by persuading Abraham to get a second wife. She was surprised and angry when Hagar acted out. When the other son Ishmael was a teenager acting out of envy and pride, she put him out so that he wouldn't be a bad influence on her son, Isaac!

But what did Elohim think about Ishmael?

In this situation, God agreed with Sarah. Sarah had made some mistakes, but she was right to protect her young son from persecution and mocking that could potentially affect him for the rest of his life. God showed up to Abraham and told him to listen to his wife and put Hagar and Ishmael out. This was only for the purpose of protecting Isaac, the covenant son.

Hagar and Ishmael ended up all by themselves in the desert again, put out from their family. Hagar was so sad that after she finished the water bottle, she left her teenage son in the bush to die, because she didn't want to see it happen.

But remember, God was the one that gave Ishmael his name. Ishmael means "heard by God".

God gave Ishmael a promise that He would be heard!

> *Genesis 21:* ¹⁷ *And **God heard the voice**
> **of the lad;** and the angel of **God called to**
> **Hagar out of heaven**, and said unto her,
> What aileth thee, Hagar? fear not; for **God**
> **hath heard the voice of the lad where he is**.
> ¹⁸ Arise, lift up the lad, and hold him in thine
> hand; for **I will make him a great nation**.*

When Hagar and Ishmael were ready to die, Elohim saw them, heard them, and gave them a blessing. Ishmael developed hunting skills in the wilderness, and Elohim made Ishmael into a great nation.

Your Heavenly Father sees. Your Heavenly Father hears. Your Heavenly Father cares.

To those who have any level of fatherlessness in their lives, from divorce, to abuse, to abandonment; it wasn't your fault that you were born into a bad situation. But your ABBA Father hears you.

God has given you a special gift in prayer. If you cry out to Him, He will deliver you. Cry out to your Father in Heaven today!

What can we learn from Ishmael and Israel?

- Ishmael means "heard by Elohim".
- Those that came from bad situations of sexual sin, strife, abandonment, or separation are **still seen**, and **heard**, and **cared for** by their Father in Heaven.
- When they cry out to Him, He will hear them.
- Ishmael's brother Isaac had a son named Jacob, who became Israel. Israel means "ruled by Elohim".
- Ishmael and Israel (from Isaac's son Jacob) are both nations that came from Abraham and were both blessed by God.

- Though their lineage was separated for a purpose; in the end, Ishmael must unite with Israel.
- In the Messiah, the descendants of Ishmael and the descendants Israel can be reunited into one family again!
- Those that are "heard by God" must join together with those that are "ruled by God."
- Those that have a special gift in prayer must become one with those that know how to follow God's rules.
- When they submit themselves to God's Commandments and His order, they can walk in His greatest blessings.

OUR FATHER'S FAMILY CULTURE

We need to get **FAMILY**-AR with our Father's <u>House Rules</u> and our Father's <u>Family Culture</u>!

One of the most exciting things the Holy Spirit has taught me in the past few years is learning more about my Father in Heaven and His Commandments.

Normally in most churches, they focus more on Jesus the Son of God, and act as if everything in the Old Testament is irrelevant. But my mind has been blown the more I learn about how consistent the Son was with Honoring His Father's culture, His Father's rules, and His Father's house; even as He invited Gentiles into the Kingdom.

No, I'm not talking about the law of circumcision or the covenant agreement that Elohim made with Abraham. I'm also not talking about the feast days of Israel, or the covenant made through Moses. I'm talking about the actual will and testimony of our Father in Heaven, the 10 Commandments, and the Moral laws of Liberty and Love (Romans 11:19, Deuteronomy 5:22).

The Ten Commandments are not meant to give us salvation. Only Jesus's sacrifice on the cross can do that. However, the Law is a schoolmaster that leads us to Christ (Galatians 3:24). The Law of the Father is meant to minister death to our sinful flesh, so that our spirits can be made alive by the Holy Ghost (2 Corinthians 3:7,8)!

We aren't trying to circumcise everybody's foreskin like the Judaizers were doing in Galatia (Galatians 5:12); we want to have circumcised hearts to Yah's ways. We aren't trying to force everyone to keep Mosaic feast days and ceremonial sabbaths like the Judaizers were doing in Colossae (Colossians 2:16). In the New Covenant, Yah sends His Holy Spirit to set His people apart in holiness.

We have found out that the Law of the YAH is perfect, converting the soul. The testimony of YAH is pure, making the simple wise (Psalms 19:7). When we are filled with the Spirit, our minds become subject to the Law of God (Romans 8:4,7).

It all started with trying to keep the Creation Sabbath on the seventh day of the week when I was in my early twenties. I realized that God was smarter than me, and I wanted to create a personal, and later, family culture of rest to enjoy the benefits of His wisdom. I learned more and more as the years went on.

A few years ago, I learned the history of why the Sabbath was changed to Sunday, who did it, how evil they were, and how they abused and persecuted both disciples and Jews who honored the Sabbath.

This made me realize how powerful God's Commandments were, and how desperate the devil was to eliminate the power of obedience to God's Commandments.

This put me on a journey of learning about the second Commandment against graven images and idolatry. The understanding of Yah's heart towards the exclusivity of covenant love opened the door for a higher level of revelation on what Jesus taught about lust, divorce, and remarriage as adultery in the eyes of the Most High.

This journey down the narrow path of obedience hasn't been easy. Obedience has opened several new streams of revelation, action, and power that I never even would have noticed if I had not gotten started. I know the devil hates it because of the tremendous power in the Father's will and testimony. One thing about me: if the devil hates something—my goal is to love it! My goal is to be One with the Father and the Son!

The Father and the Son are One!

When you join into Christ, you enter in the Father's House. This is why Jesus said: "In my FATHER'S HOUSE are MANY MANSIONS, if it were not so, I wouldn't have told you. Behold, I go to prepare a place for you!"

In Hebrew culture, families stayed together. YAHUAH owned the land of Israel, and property was handed down from generation to generation. There were no real estate tycoons that could amass property unto themselves. Every 50 years, there was a jubilee year where debts were forgiven and property had to be returned to the family it was assigned to.

When you married into a family, you joined that family's culture, and you joined the family business, and you went to the family property. When you married the son, he built you a house on the property of his own father!

GOD is not changing His family culture for us; we are supposed to enter His Culture thru our Covenant with His Son!

The Son of God made this ABUNDANTLY CLEAR when He said:

> *Matthew 7: 21 Not every one that saith unto me, Lord, Lord, shall enter into the kingdom of heaven; but he that DOETH THE WILL OF MY FATHER which is in heaven.*

22 MANY WILL SAY TO ME in that day,
Lord, Lord, have we not prophesied in thy
name? and in thy name have cast out devils?
and in thy name done many wonderful works?
23 And then will I profess unto them,
I NEVER KNEW YOU: depart from
me, ye that WORK INIQUITY.

If you rebel against the WILL and TESTAMENT of His Father in Heaven (the Two Tablets, the 10 Commandments, the Law of Liberty), and if you work the LAWLESSNESS and INIQUITY of this world system (Babylon/anti-Christ), Jesus will profess to you:

"I never knew you, I never married you, we did not consummate the Covenant, and I don't even KNOW you!"

Jesus is not changing any of the Father's 10 Commandments! The 10 Commandments of the Father and the two Great Commandments go hand in hand. The first five commandments show us how to love God with our whole heart, soul, mind, and strength. The second five commandments show us how to love our neighbors as ourselves. All His Commandments are based on LOVE!

Do we really know our Father in Heaven? Do we even know His Family Culture?

Jesus taught us further how His Father's family culture works in what I call the "Kingdom Constitution." It's found in Matthew chapters 5, 6, and 7.

Sometimes we publicize our prayer, fasting, and almsgiving because we don't have the leadership of our Father. He rewards us for doing those in secret (Matthew 6).

Other times, we privatize repentance, holiness, judgment, and the wisdom of God because we don't have the leadership of our Father. He rewards us for putting those out in the open and glorifying Him (Matthew 5).

There are so many mindsets that we get from this world that are totally different from the culture of our Father in Heaven. We have to ask ourselves:

Are we people pleasers or do we want to please our Father in Heaven?

Are we bringing our fatherlessness into the Family of God, or are we being healed and learning our Father's voice?

Reconnecting with Your Father's House

Forgive those that have wronged you so that your Father in heaven can forgive you too for what you've done wrong (Matthew 6:15). **Then, repent for your own rebellion** against His Wisdom.

Your Father in Heaven will put you in a family, and place your family in a called out, New Covenant Ecclesia (a.k.a. Congregation, a.k.a. Assembly) that will simply do His will and obey <u>His Commandments</u> and <u>His Son's Commandments</u>.

- You will learn how to Worship the Father in **Spirit and in Truth**.
- You will learn how to Worship the Father in **Decency and in Order.**
- You will gain eternal fruit and rewards on **Earth AND in HEAVEN**.

> *Psalm 68:6 God setteth the **solitary in families**:*
> *he bringeth out those which are bound with*
> *chains: but **the rebellious dwell in a dry land**.*

*Revelation 14:[12] Here is the patience of
the SAINTS: here are they that keep the
commandments of God, and the **faith of Jesus**.*

How to Restore Your Kingdom Family

1. Forgive those that have wronged you every single time it comes up in your mind, 70x7 (490) times per day. This will renew your spirit and free you from any bitterness.
2. If possible, open any broken lines of communication with your physical father and mother. Honor them any way you can, and you will be blessed by the Most High.
3. Repent for rebellion against any godly but imperfect authorities and submit yourself to them. God blesses us through imperfect people. Don't let personality weaknesses, mistakes, or the devil's devices steal you away from God's blessings for you.
4. Repent and ask God for forgiveness for being ignorant of God's commandments in the past.
5. Pray that God would heal you from any church hurt you have suffered, and that He would lead you to a congregation that keeps the commandments of God, and the faith of Jesus.
6. Join a congregation that keeps the commandments of God and the New Covenant faith of Jesus. Get familiar with your Kingdom family culture.

Study and write out the commandments of Jesus and the Ordinances of a New Covenant Congregation. Our ministry website: www. h2h2hop.com/hop and my blog www.sospression.com are two good places to start your search.

YOUR FATHER IN HEAVEN WILL RESTORE AND EXPAND YOUR KINGDOM FAMILY

Loneliness can be a big problem in our hearts if our families are dysfunctional and scattered due to lack of high-character leadership from our fathers. It can get even worse when so-called spiritual leaders turn out unqualified, abusive, or selfish. But God still sets the solitary in families (Psalms 68:6). That's His job!

We may be tempted to turn to sin, selfishness, rebellion, or independence to make it on our own and make a "name for ourselves." We may be tempted to turn to food, alcohol, drug, sex, or media addictions to numb the pain of losing someone we trusted.

However, those will never be the answers that our hearts need. Our answer will always be found in our relationship with our Father in Heaven. We must allow Him to heal us, mend our hearts, and show us His Family Culture.

We must allow His Son Jesus to be our Surgeon and our Shepherd; removing sin and rebellion from our hearts, and restoring us to our place in His flock.

Chapter 7

Father to the Fatherless:
RESTORE YOUR CONFIDENCE
AND SELF-WORTH!

*Malachi 4:⁵ Behold, I will send you Elijah the prophet before the
coming of the great and dreadful day of the Lord: ⁶ And he shall turn
the heart of the fathers to the children, and the heart of the children
to their fathers, lest I come and smite the earth with a curse.*

Fathers, the number one way to turn your heart to your children is to love their mother.

Their mother is half-of them, so by loving their mother you give them the opportunity to see themselves as worthy of love. You give them self-worth.

One of the biggest things I respect about my father is that he never abused his wife, my mother. He was stern at times to us children, and in control of the house, but he was never violent. I really don't even remember him raising his voice at her.

I remember one time he got mad at somebody else that he was doing business with, and he threw the phone in anger at the guy he was talking too. He humbled himself and repented to us as little children for his display of wrath in front of us. That's the type of character that he showed to us.

I'm sure that my parents had a normal relationship with ups and downs, but they never gave up their covenant. They stuck together, and I am thankful for it. I am blessed for it. It gave me a good foundation of confidence and self-worth.

It's common knowledge that when parents are divorced, the children are more tempted towards violence and sexual sin. What could cause these responses? These behaviors come from the base sinful nature, but they are amplified by a lack of self-worth.

Multiple examples in Genesis show that a lack of self-worth leads to both violence and sexual sin. Then sexual sin leads to more violence and more sexual sin in the next generations.

The first murder was Cain on his brother Abel. Cain's occupation (a tiller of the ground) was **different than his brother** Abel (a keeper of the sheep), but **not less important**. However, in worship of Elohim, Cain's role was to offer the tithe of his crops to Abel in exchange for a sheep to offer to Elohim. Instead of having confidence in who he was in fulfilling his role in worship, Cain decided to envy his brother Abel, which turned into a disobedient offering, and resulted in murder.

Unfortunately, Cain set a pattern for generations after himself of people that felt like they need to destroy others because they lack an understanding of their self-worth. How many children grow up feeling like they have been given a lesser calling, or a lesser talent that is not as important as someone else's?

One of Cain's great-great-great grandson's name was Lamech. He continued in Cain's ways, but he took it to the next logical step. Not only did he murder another man, he also rewarded himself for that accomplishment by taking two wives. Then, he wrote a song about it!

> *Genesis 4:23 And Lamech said unto his wives,*
> *Adah and Zillah, Hear my voice; ye wives of*
> *Lamech, hearken unto my speech: for I have*
> *slain a man to my wounding, and a young*
> *man to my hurt. 24 If Cain shall be avenged*
> *sevenfold, truly Lamech seventy and sevenfold.*

The first murderer in history is someone who didn't want to give tithes or first fruits to a shepherd because they weren't confident in their own calling. The second murderer in history is also the first person in the Scriptures with two wives.

This shows me that a lack of self-worth leads to violence and to sexual sin. The accounts of Cain and Lamech in Genesis 4 shows the link between lack of self-worth, sexual sin, and violence.

A couple chapters later in Genesis 6, Noah's flood happens as God's response to those same two things: **sexual sin** and **violence**!

The backdrop of Genesis 4:23 shows us that Genesis 6:1–4 is <u>not about fallen angels</u>—it's about fallen HUMANS with unbridled lust and violence, which creates <u>fatherless children with desires to be greater than others</u> (giants/superstars).

Many fatherless children were born into lust instead of covenant love. These fatherless children feel a great internal sense of rejection, which creates an unhealthy sense of envy, pride, and competition for greatness that comes from a lack of self-worth.

This unhealthy sense of competition leads to violence, psychological and physical. Then generation after generation continues in the cycles of violence and the repetition of lust.

Competition and Rejection Harms Our Souls

If I reject my children's mother, I'm partly rejecting them. This could cause them to reject any fatherly wisdom from me and can also cause them to lack confidence in who they are and how they are made.

Take basketball for example: if I teach my sons and correct them on how to shoot or dribble, do they see it as competition or as me helping them be better? They are not threatened by my correction because I am their father. They know I'm trying to help them be better than me one day.

But if I reject them, they will feel threatened, and they will learn to respond to threats with violence.

Simple and fun things in life can turn into brutal competition and wrath when there are deficiencies in our souls. If you've ever seen guys curse each other out at a basketball court you know what I'm talking about.

I have to brag a little about my son. I took him to a basketball gym a couple weeks ago, and I went to another room for a few minutes. During that time, a kid punched him in the jaw for playing tough defense.

What I am excited about is even though my son was very angry, he didn't let pride cause him to retaliate. Since I was there, he came and reported it to me, and we reported it to the manager of the facility instead of hitting him back. It was recorded on video, so there was evidence of what happened for disciplinary reasons.

I do teach him that it's okay to defend himself, and especially to defend his younger siblings. However, the decision he made in that moment showed amazing maturity to me. How foolish would it be to fight somebody over a basketball game? The only reason you would escalate a situation like that is foolish pride.

I was extremely joyful that my son had enough self-confidence and trust in authority to de-escalate and report that situation instead of getting a cheap hit on a kid that he was younger, but slightly bigger than.

There have been other times when he didn't always make the best decision. There are times when he has defended himself or his little brothers, and there are times when he has de-escalated and spoken to authorities. I try to love him through his mistakes, and I love to see him walk in wisdom whether it's in self-defense, or in de-escalation.

Putting Non-Competitive Confidence in our Daughters

Take my daughters for example. If I tell them they are beautiful, do they take it as if I'm lusting after them? No, because they know that I love their mother. I am complementing them in purity, therefore, their beauty is pure.

My oldest daughter Lily is five-years old; she often tells her mother that she doesn't want to get too dressed up for church. She doesn't want to hear other people to tell her how beautiful she is. She knows she is beautiful, so she doesn't feel the pressure to display it, especially in the presence of God. Nobody taught her this, this came out of her heart.

But if I reject my daughters or am absent, they will develop a desire to be lusted after, which will lead them into vanity and seduction. Their beauty will be weaponized against others and eventually against their own selves.

Weaponized beauty "slays" men by turning them into victims, manipulated by seduction.

Weaponized beauty "enslaves" women by stealing their confidence by causing them to desire false standards of beauty and vanity that they can **never actually attain or retain** for more than a few quick years. We see the results of this every day in modern culture.

Manly strength and **womanly beauty** are natural and good, given to us by God. I'm not preaching against what is natural!

What I'm saying is that we need to de-emphasize strength and beauty, and start to create family cultures that emphasize, wisdom, obedience, and the Fear of YAHUAH!

We must learn to give verbal praise and take pleasure when our young men fear the Lord and keep His commandments more than in their strength and athleticism.

> *Psalms 147: [10] He delighteth not in the strength of the horse: **he taketh not pleasure in the legs of a man**. [11] The LORD taketh pleasure in them that fear him, in those that hope in his mercy.*

We must learn to give verbal praise and take pleasure when our young women fear the Lord and keep his commandments more than in their beauty and fashion.

> *Proverbs 31: [30] Favour is deceitful, and **beauty is vain**: but a woman that feareth the LORD, she shall be praised.*

Doing this on purpose will help us be free from youthful lusts, the deceitfulness of sin and the corrupted world system.

Recognizing the Iniquities that Come from our Wounds

Whenever fatherlessness causes us to constantly feel competition and rejection—even where there is none…we must be healed by our Father in Heaven!

Sometimes our iniquities come from a lack of self-worth from our fathers:

- Our anger and wrath can come from seeing correction as a form of competition or rejection instead of love.
- Our pride and vanity are ways of overcompensating for a lack of confidence.
- Our lust and gluttony are overcompensating for the way we devalue our bodies.
- Our fear and doubt can come from how we don't think we deserve protection or reward.
- Our rebellion and bitterness can come from feeling like we are on our own with no one to provide for us.

We tend to use these iniquities to overcompensate for the holes we have in our heart.

We choose our **deceptions** according to our **deficiencies**. INIQUITY (in-equity) is the opposite of INTEGRITY.

Your Abba Father Has Given You Everything You Need

If you have a low self-worth or confidence because of your father's separation from your mother, please know that you have a Father in heaven who loves you!

You are not deficient in anything! Your Father in heaven has given you everything you need, and He will never leave you. You are complete in Him!

Jesus came to reveal ABBA Father to the Jews that thought they already knew Him—but they didn't. Once you have seen Jesus, you have seen the Father!

The Father and the Son have an unbroken covenant, and when you **join into this covenant** with Christ, you can be made whole, full, complete, mature, with INTEGRITY, and with no deficiencies.

Say it with me: "I am NOT deficient in ANYTHING, **I am COMPLETE in Christ!**"

Speak it. Believe it. Do it! **You will be made WHOLE!**

How to Restore Your Confidence and Self-Worth

1. Embrace your **natural strength** and your **natural beauty** given to you by God. This will give you a new level of **non-competitive confidence**.
2. Honor God by honoring the genetics, gifts, and talents that God gave you through your father and your mother. When you honor your **father and mother**, you will be amazed at the results you will have by using what God gave you through them to succeed in life.
3. Repent from all the iniquities that come from rejection or wounds in your soul. Find your pride, lust, envy, fears, wrath, rebellion, and bitterness. Tell them to leave and replace them with forgiveness 70x7 (490) times per day. Replace them with obedience.
4. Reject the excessive competitions of strength and beauty in modern Greco-Romanized culture. Use your life to **emphasize wisdom**, character, prudence, and natural productivity, instead of youthful lusts. Get out of the Greco-Roman "brat race."
5. De-emphasize pride and vanity. **Chase fruitfulness**, humility, modesty, moderation, and service, instead of covetousness and deceitful riches. Get out of the American "rat race."
6. Give **Thanks Out Loud** and **Speak with Confidence** about what God has done for you both spiritually and naturally. Give God thanks for all things, **at all times**!

YOUR CREATOR WILL RESTORE YOUR CONFIDENCE AND SELF-WORTH!

Our Father in Heaven is the giver of every good gift that we have. He is the Father of lights (James 1:17). He gave us the light that sparks our soul into life, and He gives us the Light of eternal life in His Son!

Two of the other greatest gifts He has given us on earth are our father and mother. Our physical, mental, and spiritual genetics come directly from our father and mother! We must thank our Creator for our father and mother and seek to honor them by using what Elohim has given us through them.

Restoring your confidence and self-worth will come from knowing who you are and using what you have been given from above. There's no competition for you, because everything you have comes from heaven through your father and mother.

Even if your father and mother didn't treat you well or do everything right, there is still hope for you. With the power of your Father in Heaven, you can restore everything good that He put inside of you. You can also get rid of everything bad, and move forward in confidence; knowing that you are worthy of God's best!

Chapter 8

Father to the Fatherless: RESTORE YOUR LOVE/ COVENANT FAITHFULNESS!

Because iniquity shall abound, the Love of many shall wax cold.—Jesus (Matthew 24:12).

t's going to be a sad judgement day for a lot of folks when they find out that God defines "love" very differently than the smooth jazz station, the R&B station, the country station, the old school soul & Motown music channels, the romance novels and the chick flicks.

What is Love?

Contrary to popular opinion, Yah's definition of mercy and love is not based on emotion. The Hebrew definition of Love is simply "Covenant Faithfulness." Love = Faithfulness to Covenant.

The Scriptures teach a Foundational Understanding of Covenant that is a backdrop for everything we see in the earth from nature itself, to the people and families in the earth.

What is a Covenant?

It is an agreement or commitment made with our mouth.

The culture of the Scriptures is heavy on integrity, being faithful to your word. We serve a God who does everything by speaking words. This whole earth and all of the heavens hang on His Word.

Words are very important. The integrity, weight, and faithfulness of our words are very important.

God is not going to adjust reality or rewrite the Scriptures to fit with the vain and flaky entertainment-based culture of our day.

The very definition of MERCY is: Covenant Faithfulness.

Without Covenant, there is NO LOVE.

Love is DEFINED BY COVENANT.

Look it up: mercy in Hebrew is "chesed", (Strong's number 02617.)

Babylon/Greco Roman/American Love is based on feelings and emotions, but YAHUAH'S Love is based on COVENANT and being Faithful to the Words of our Mouth.

Is your "LOVE" based on EMOTIONS or COMMITTMENT?

What is Faithfulness?

Faithfulness is the lack of a difference between what we do and what comes out of our mouths. We should do what we say. **Mouth – Actions = Zero.**

In the old covenant, you had to keep all your oaths and pledges. It was so serious that people were killed over completely unnecessary oaths, pledges, and vows.

In the new covenant, Jesus told us to stop making oaths and pledges altogether! Just say yes or no. That's how powerful our words are. Our mouths can get us in the most trouble. We are to let our yay be yay, and our nay be nay.

What is Iniquity?

Iniquity is when something in our heart or soul is not equal. It is unstable because it is <u>not what YAH designed it to be</u>.

When our words and actions are not based on the logic of truth, it does not compute. Iniquity is a glitch in our spiritual software.

Iniquity gives us **Fear** instead of **Trust and Faith**.
Iniquity gives us **Lust** instead of **Thankfulness and Self-Control**.
Iniquity gives us **Pride** instead of **Modesty and Contentment**.
Iniquity gives us **Envy** instead of **Diligence and Generosity**.
Iniquity gives us **Rebellion** instead of **Patience and Submission to Authority**.
Iniquity gives us **Bitterness** instead of **Repentance and Forgiveness**.

Iniquity (in-equity) is the opposite of **Integrity**.

Integrity is when our heart and soul is balanced, solid, and equal. We are faithful to the words of our mouth, which are based on the solid Truth of God's Law and Creation Design.

Our hearts and souls must be made complete with integrity to walk in covenant faithfulness—which IS LOVE.

Why is this important? The first covenant that every human literally comes out of is the covenant between our father and mother.

Sometimes there is no covenant, and the relationship is based on iniquity (in-equity) that leads to fornication or adultery.

Sometimes the **integrity of the covenant** is **broken by the violence of divorce (Malachi 2:16).**

Jesus was talking about the last days when He said: "MANY shall be offended, and shall BETRAY one another, and shall HATE one another. And many FALSE PROPHETS shall arise and shall DECEIVE MANY. And **because INIQUITY shall abound, the LOVE of many shall wax cold**. But he that shall endure to the end, the same shall be saved." Matthew 24:10–13

In this wicked and adulterous generation, we live in an evil time of lies, sorcery, theft, murder, and fornication.

Lies are being pushed, promoted, and published by every level of government, media, and society. Iniquity, hypocrisy, injustice, and adultery is being displayed on every screen.

When we are surrounded by iniquities (in-equities), broken covenants, unfaithfulness, and a lack of integrity, sometimes we can allow it to affect us.

It can make us think that God doesn't care that much.
It can make us think that God doesn't keep track of our commitments.
It can make us think that God won't reward us for our faithfulness.
It can make us think that we will get away with lying and in-equities without consequence, because we see so much iniquity around us.

PLEASE don't let your Covenant Faithfulness (the **Integrity of your Mouth and Actions**) aka LOVE grow cold in this evil time.

Love hurts, love takes courage, and a true friend is Faithful to speak the truth instead of lying (Proverbs 27:6).

Don't let this evil time make your heart grow cold towards REAL LOVE.

Don't let the broken Covenant of your father and mother continue to break the integrity of your soul.

Be healed and made whole by your Father in Heaven!

With His strength, you CAN keep your promises and your integrity.

Your Father in Heaven will NEVER leave you or forsake you.

He is faithful when we are not faithful. He cannot deny Himself (2 Timothy 2:13).

So, with His strength, you will stay FAITHFUL in LOVE to the promises you made to Him, to your spouse, to your family, and to the people He placed in your life.

Malachi 4: 5 Behold, I will send you Elijah the prophet before the coming of the great and dreadful day of the Lord: 6 And he shall turn the heart of the fathers to the children, and the heart of the children to their fathers, lest I come and smite the earth with a curse.

How Did Covenant Love get turned into Cold Love?

It was 1989 when my family moved from Chicago to Detroit. My Dad got a job working for Ford. I remember hearing bad things about Detroit, but I couldn't see it! The neighborhood we moved into was clean, and there wasn't trash all over the streets for me to clean up on Saturday mornings like I did when we lived in Chicago.

Fast forward to 2011, I had lived in Detroit for over 20 years. I moved back to the city after college and had prayed for the city for over 10 years. Learning more and more about the prophetic history of Detroit had my wife and I leading prayer meetings where we not only prayed about the city but discovered certain things about the city that needed to be repented of.

From 2012 to 2016, we did prayer tours around the city where we went to certain historic and prophetically significant locations to speak the Word of God with authority and pray over them. But the revelation that opened everything came when we did a tour of the Motown Museum.

I never visited the museum my whole life in Detroit, but as we walked around it with other house of prayer leaders, things became clear about the Motown Blueprint.

The city of Detroit has an industrial calling, and a lot of what was created in Detroit ends up changing the world. Even things that are not invented in Detroit become mass duplicable from Detroit. From the auto industry to Techno music, Detroit's calling for massive impact has been felt all over the earth.

There are many things that Detroit is known for, but one of the biggest things is the Motown Music "hit factory." It cannot be overstated how much impact Motown music has had on the world. Motown the label didn't invent music, but it industrialized the making of hit records for massive impact.

The Motown sound crossed age, ethnicity, and cultural barriers. Even the Beatles gave credit to Motown for their sound. Many other genres and labels patterned themselves after Motown's formula. Motown is known as the music that changed America![1]

The Motown Blueprint

What was the first hit song from Motown? It's called "Money (That's What I Want)." It was released in 1959[2] and it was so popular, that it was later recorded by the Beatles and the Rolling Stones.

This was a song that celebrated the love for money! But the Scriptures teach us that **covetousness** (the love for money) is **idolatry** (Colossians 3:5).

What was the second hit song from Motown? It's called "Gotta Shop Around". This song was released in 1960, and it contains instructions from a mother to her son to try many different women before committing to marry his bride.

Contrary to Smokey, my mommy told me the opposite! She told me that having many different girlfriends cheapened the value of having a wife, and it ends up just being practice for divorce and adultery.

In 1960 (the same year that "Gotta Shop Around" was released), 33% of Black children in America were not living with two parents. In 1988, that number rose to 61%. During that same time, Black children born to an unmarried mother rose from 23% to over 60%.[3]

In 1958, the divorce rate for Americans was 2.1 per 1000. The largest increase in the divorce rate for all Americans happened in the 1960s and 1970s. In the late 70s, it went up to 5.3, then by 1989 it went to 4.7.

After 1989, divorce rates continued to decline, but only because less people were choosing to get married in the first place.[4] The music changed America.

Essentially, Motown took youth that were called to worship God from the churches and paid them to give their sound and talent to songs that were about idolatry, adultery, and fake, emotion-based love.

The quick and adaptive mass duplication of this process impacted the world by effectively doubling divorce, doubling fatherlessness, and causing an overall decline in covenant marriage in one generation.

Are there other economic, technological, and legislative factors that impacted marriages in the 30 years that passed between 1959 and 1989? Of course, there were. But the Scripture shows that covenant love is as strong as death (Song of Solomon 8:6). The **only** thing that can destroy covenant love is the process of false prophets spreading deception and iniquity to **replace covenant love with cold love.**

When we give our worshippers and prophets to industry to become entertainers and hypocrites (actors) for idolatry and adultery, it introduces a fake, cold love that brings long-term destruction to our covenant love, our families, and our children.

> *Matthew 24: [11] And many false prophets*
> *shall rise, and shall deceive many.*
> *[12] And **because iniquity shall abound, the***
> ***love of many shall wax cold.***
> *[13] But he that shall endure unto the end, the same shall be saved.*

Many Waters Can't Quench Love!

The Hebrew family in America endured slavery, Jim Crow, lynchings, and miseducation. None of those things broke us.

Those things had an effect, but never destroyed our families permanently. We've always bounced back through our character and integrity. How were we able to create such great communities after slavery, and Jim Crow, and lynchings?

We even bounced back after community massacres like Black Wall Street, Rosewood, and Margaret Sanger's Eugenics based "Negro Project" to create successful families and communities. Our families always bounced back!

What destroyed the Hebrew family long-term? What finally got past our covenant love?

1. Motown Music Factory: **Self-Sponsored** corruption of our worship and marriages set stage for a culture of idolatry, adultery, and divorce, leading to fatherlessness.
2. Sexual Revolution/Birth Control/Abortion Industry: **Business-Sponsored** destruction of Covenant faithfulness, death culture curse released.
3. Blaxploitation Pimp Culture Films: **Entertainment-Induced** culture of laziness, degradation, and idle dreams.
4. Welfare Industry: **Government-Sponsored** break up of families, removing fathers from children.
5. Drug Industry and War on Drugs: **Government-Sponsored** destruction of communities by trafficking drugs into our communities, and then declaring war on drugs to stimulate the warfare economy.

The Hebrew family was not destroyed by slavery, lynchings, or massacres. It was destroyed by music from false prophets that change our idea of love from a covenant with God into a feeling and a vibe.

Even the other economic and government factors that helped destroy our families would have been completely ineffective without our own false prophets giving them entrance and permission.

*   If we had kept our covenant love—to worship God instead of money.
*   If we had kept our covenant love—to marry one wife instead of "shopping around,"

Then none of the imported drugs, welfare checks, or blaxploitation films would have been able to destroy half of our families. Our self-sponsored corruption of worship and covenant love is opened those doors.

Returning to YAH's Heart: Covenant Love

Even to this day, Detroit has the highest percentage of single women of any major city in the U.S., and the 2nd highest percentage of single men [5]. Overall, Detroit leads the nation in single people with 70.8%.

It's not a sin to be single, but it is **idolatry** to break your covenant of exclusive worship to God, and it is **adultery** to break a covenant with your spouse before death by divorcing them and marrying someone else.

Over the last couple of generations, there were so many marriages ending in divorce, that marriage has become a less popular option in general. I do not think it's a coincidence that the city that led a massive promotion of turning covenant worship into idolatry and turning covenant love into emotion is now leading the nation in lack of covenant marriages.

The spiritual power of Motown literally changed the world in one generation. They sold love, but it became cold love. It's been said that as Detroit goes, so goes the world. Detroit has influence all over the world, so we also need to lead the world in repentance.

Everyone in the world has to follow in repentance has to be from idolatry, (violating our covenant with God), and from adultery (violating our covenants with our spouses, divorce and remarriage). We must repent from false worship, covetousness, fornication, and adultery.

Remember: **covenant love can never be destroyed, only replaced with cold love** through the iniquity that comes from false prophets.

Just like covenant love can be replaced by false prophets, the iniquity of cold love can be replaced by true prophets that come to return Yah's people to His heart by keeping His Commandments.

If we want to rescue our covenant marriages, our families, and be a help to the fatherless, this will only happen in its fullness when we return to the COMMANDMENTS of GOD and the FAITH of JESUS.

We need to return to **covenant love**!

> *Song of Solomon 8:7*
> ***Many waters cannot quench love****, neither can the
> floods drown it: if a man would give all the substance of
> his house for love, it would utterly be contemned.*

- All the tribulation and trouble this world can throw at me can't quench Covenant Love!
- I don't need the riches that men can offer me because I have Covenant Love!

LOVE IS A COMITMENT TO GOD

Is your "LOVE" based on EMOTIONS or COMMITTMENT?

> *1 John 4:10* ***HEREIN IS LOVE****, not that
> we loved God, but that he loved us, and sent
> his Son to be the propitiation for our sins.*

LOVE IS: GOD SACRIFICING HIS SON'S BODY, BLOOD, AND PAIN FOR OUR SINS. HE SUFFERED WHAT HE DIDN'T DESERVE.

> *1 John 5:3 For* ***THIS IS THE LOVE OF
> GOD****, that we keep his commandments: and
> **his commandments are not grievous.***

LOVE IS: US LOVING HIM BACK BY GUARDING AND OBEYING HIS COMMANDMENTS. HIS COMMANDMENTS ARE LOVE—NOT LIES

John 15:10 If ye keep my commandments,
ye shall ABIDE IN MY LOVE; even as
I have kept my Father's commandments,
and ABIDE IN HIS LOVE.

Keeping the Son's Commandments automatically puts you within the Father's Commandments, which causes you to ABIDE in the LOVE of both the Son (Yahusha) AND the Father (Yahuah).

How to Restore Your Love/Covenant Faithfulness

1. Join the New Covenant with God in Heaven through repentance from sin against His Commandments, and faith and obedience to His Son Jesus Christ. Repent from all forms of idolatry and put God first over everything.
2. Repent from all forms of adultery. Honor your original marriage covenant if your original spouse is still alive. Repent and forgive, reconcile, and return if they are willing. Remain faithful to your covenant even if your spouse is not. You are accountable for your own actions. Get Counseling from a Pastor who teaches the Commandments of Jesus.
3. Develop the character of staying faithful to your word and leading by example in faithfulness. Psalm 15, Psalm 24, and Psalm 101 are three great Psalms to study regarding how to develop the integrity and leadership that God is looking for.
4. Simplify your life to the things that are important and productive. Minimize your distractions from entertainers and hypocrites. The eyes of a fool are in the ends of the earth (Proverbs 17:24).
5. Love the people around you, love your neighbor, and love the people that God has placed in your life.

Bonus: Study the Natural Laws of Creation. The Natural laws of the Most High will help simplify your life and help you to avoid the iniquities that lead to greater sins. Our ministry website: www.h2h2hop.com/hop and my blog: www.sospression.com are good places to start your search for Scriptural references.

THE MOST HIGH WILL HEAL OUR HEARTS AND RESTORE COVENANT LOVE!

In a healthy culture, fatherlessness is the result of tragedy and covenant faithfulness aka love is never broken.

In a wicked and perverse culture, fatherlessness is a result of fornication, divorce, adultery, and idolatry.

We must return to a culture of covenant faithfulness if we want to bring healing to our generation. Covenant love stabilizes and transforms families. Communities are then positively transformed for the through the tangible acts of love and service given against the backdrop of stable families.

We must reject a hypocrite culture based on performers and entertainers. This creates a fake form of love based on the iniquities of lust, greed, pride, vanity, and coolness.

We must embrace a kingdom culture with the righteousness of God based on tangible acts of hospitality, generosity, kindness, and covenant love.

References:

1. Haider, A. (2019). Motown: The Music That Changed America. British Broadcasting Corporation (BBC). https://www.bbc.com/culture/article/20190109-motown-the-music-that-changed-america

2.   Rohter, L. (2013). For a Classic Motown Song About
     Money, Credit is What He Wants. The New York Times.
     https://www.nytimes.com/2013/09/01/arts/music/for-
     a-classic-motown-song-about-money-credit-is-what-he-
     wants.html

3.   Ellwood, D.T. Crane, J. (1990). Family Change Among
     Black Americans: What Do We Know? Journal of
     Economic Perspectives, Volume 4, Number 4
     https://pubs.aeaweb.org/doi/pdf/10.1257/jep.4.4.65

4.   Olito, F. (2019) How the divorce rate has changed over
     the last 150 years. Insider Inc.
     https://www.insider.com/divorce-rate-changes-over-time-
     2019-1#in-the-60s-the-rate-slowly-started-to-climb-again-
     ending-the-decade-with-a-new-high-32-annual-divorces-
     for-every-1000-americans-9

5.   Neal. (2022). As A Single Player Game, We Wanted To
     Know The Suburbs With The Most Singles. Solitaire Bliss.
     https://www.solitairebliss.com/blog/
     single-player-game-and-suburbs-with-singles

Chapter 9

Father to the Fatherless:
RESTORE YOUR BOUNDARIES
AND RESPONSIBILITIES!

Fathers Set Boundaries and Responsibilities

Fathers **know our design**; they **show us our gifts and talents**. A father is the first authority in your life to give you a role and a **responsibility according to your gift, talent, and place in a group**. He does this in the family household, which should be the first and safest place for you to learn how to think and act.

When a healthy father does this for you, it's **not based on manipulation; it's based on design**. It's not **a form of abuse**, it's giving you the **right opportunity you need to grow**.

A healthy father does not cross your boundaries; **he sets boundaries for you** and makes sure no one in the whole EARTH can cross them without dealing with him!

In a perfect world, our earthly father should be someone who shows us a similar love to our Father in Heaven.

But when you don't have the blessing of an earthly father, or if you have an abusive or emotionally manipulative father—you don't learn how to properly relate to authority at a young age.

Sexually abusive, emotionally absent, or cowardly absent fathers can cause much harm to the development of innocent children. This can affect how we respond to heavenly authority, and the normal relationships we operate within our everyday life:

- When we don't honor our Creator, we rebel against our design.
- When we don't obey our King, we don't understand our role.
- When we have been abused or lied to by evil authority, we lose trust in all authority, and we learn to rebel against responsibility.

We now have a whole generation of people **in rebellion against their own design,** choosing homosexuality, lesbianism, unclean sexuality, abortion, harmful birth control, and other self-destructives.

Our brokenness has created a whole generation **in rebellion against their natural roles and responsibilities**.

> *Isaiah 24:5 The **earth also is defiled** under the inhabitants thereof; because they have transgressed **the laws**, changed **the ordinance**, broken **the everlasting covenant**.*

Un-Boundaried Childhoods have adversely affected our:

- Manhoods
- Womanhoods
- Husbandhoods
- Wifehoods
- Fatherhoods
- Motherhoods

Why? Because many have not be set in their proper roles, nor do they see the benefit of those roles in society.

Relationships are hard and boundaries are easily crossed because few people understand their roles or responsibilities. Instead of faithful communication and faithful action, our relationships are full of miscommunication, misunderstanding, rebellion, and manipulation.

Then we feel condemned, manipulated, afraid, and intimidated by the simple acts of service and obedience that we are responsible for based on our design and our role.

This affects us in our jobs, our worship, our friendships. Some of us see our simple human roles and responsibilities as manipulation and abuse because someone has crossed our boundaries or abused us in the past:

- Some men don't want to be men and be responsible servant leaders.
- Some women don't want to be women and be a help and support.
- Some pastors don't want to teach; they want to be entertainers.
- Some saints don't want to be sheep; they want to be goats, or wolf puppies, leaving the flock to follow ministries full of error and mixture.
- Some public servants don't want to serve; they want to enrich themselves by stealing.
- Some citizens don't want to obey the law; they want to violate the property of others.

Our boundaries have been crossed so much, we have learned to respond by rebelling against all common decency and order.

HURT AND POWER-HUNGRY SOULS

Violence, rebellion, seduction, and witchcraft **have become the hottest commodities** for a generation of hurting and fatherless children that feel like those are the only ways they can gain the power to protect themselves!

The popular trends of people seeking after **witchcraft power**, **violent power, rebellious power, seductive sexual power**, and **magic energy** comes from a generation that has been so abused that they feel powerless!

Their boundaries have been crossed and want the power to protect themselves. They want this power so much; they are even willing to get it from the devil.

This is so sad; it can make us feel like there is no hope.

RESTORATION IS COMING!

But there is hope! There is a God that is coming to RESTORE ALL THINGS! He will set boundaries that cannot be crossed. When Jesus returns to set things in order, all flesh will see the glory of YAHUAH!

He will set such a good example of righteousness and faithfulness that even the beasts of the field won't dare cross any boundaries with any violence!

Little infants and children will be protected by the glory and the fear of YAH rising across the whole earth:

> Isaiah 11:⁵ And **righteousness** shall be the girdle
> of his loins, and **faithfulness** the girdle of his
> reins. ⁶ The wolf also shall dwell with the lamb,
> and the leopard shall lie down with the kid;
> and the calf and the young lion and the fatling
> together; and a little child shall lead them. ⁷

And the cow and the bear shall feed; their young
ones shall lie down together: and the lion shall
eat straw like the ox. ⁸And the sucking child
shall play on the hole of the asp, and the weaned
child shall put his hand on the cockatrice' den. ⁹
They shall not hurt nor destroy in all my holy
mountain: for the earth shall be full of the
knowledge of the Lord, as the waters cover the sea.

In this prophetic, Scripture we see that when the knowledge of Yahuah comes back to the earth in its fullness:

- Wolves will dwell with lambs and won't eat them.
- Leopards will lie down with goats and won't touch them.
- Lions will dwell with cattle without a threat.
- Children will hang out with animals and be responsible for guiding them through the fields to eat.
- Cows and bears will feed together peacefully.
- Lions will eat straw just like oxen.
- Babies and toddler-aged children will play in holes of snakes and poisonous spiders without being threatened.
- When God's judgements are in the earth, no one, not even an animal will think about hurting another soul.

This is the beautiful news of the Gospel of Jesus's Kingdom!

The gospel of the kingdom is not just so that you can go to heaven. It's not just about personal salvation.

Salvation is an amazing benefit, and it is very important part of the gospel. Healing, deliverance, and being filled with the Holy Spirit is an amazing entrance! However, the gospel of the kingdom of Jesus is PRIMARILY about the restoration of the order of the KING of Kings.

The gospel of the kingdom includes the **restoration of all things**! When the King of Kings comes back to set up His order, not only will our spirits, souls, and bodies be saved, but everything in the earth will be put back into it's proper place.

When the Kingdom is restored, right relationships will be restored. When relationships are properly restored, our responsibilities become apparent, and faithfulness to our calling becomes our goal.

Let's Become the Generation that Seeks the Kingdom First

As we become a generation that embraces Repentance to Yah's 10 Commandments in the Spirit of Elijah, our prayer is that many hearts will be healed, restored, and knit back together.

As we rebuild the Tabernacle of David so we can ascend His Holy Mountain, we are working to be an example of the peace and safety that can only be found in His presence.

When we return to our original designs in our families and in our congregations as His children, our ABBA Father will set us in our proper roles and responsibilities in the Family of God.

The GOSPEL, the COMMANDMENTS, and the ORDINANCES of Jesus Christ will provide us with the LIGHT, the BLUEPRINT, and the WAY to the Complete Restoration of All Things!

When we walk in His ways, boundaries will be set, and responsibilities will be fulfilled. It will be a beautiful dream team led by the King of Kings! We will find out by experience that:

His Gospel is not condemnation—it is an Opportunity for Reconciliation.
His Commandments are not grievous—they are Light and Love.
His Ordinances are not abusive—they are Protective and Productive.

NO MORE EXCUSES!

JESUS PROVIDES Salvation, Forgiveness, Healing, Repentance, Deliverance, Maturity, Fruitfulness, Prosperity, Strength thru Suffering, and Grace through Persecution.

There are NO MORE excuses for us! We can no longer blame parents, grandparents, abusers, liars, and people who crossed our boundaries for the choices we make today!

We can't blame the government, the economy, or the media for our actions anymore.

There is a day of JUDGEMENT COMING SOON when we will pay for our words, actions, and lack of obedience in fulfilling our responsibilities towards the Most High God!

On that day of Judgement. there will be a GREAT REWARD for those of us that have submitted our hearts, hands, lips, and feet to the Kingdom of His Son Jesus!

Prepare the Way with Repentance

If fathers don't turn their hearts to the children, and children turn their hearts back to the fathers, God will come and curse the earth (Malachi 4:6).

But if fathers turn their hearts back to children, and the disobedient turn back to the wisdom of the just, the spirit of Elijah will Restore ALL Things, and we will be prepared to see the Lord and King Jesus Christ Return to the Earth and bring His Peace (Luke 1:17).

How to Restore Your Boundaries and Responsibilities:

1. Forgive your earthly father for anytime he failed to set boundaries of protection around you.
2. Repent for anytime you rebelled against your father's wisdom and instruction that was designed to give you the boundaries of protection and guidance.
3. Call out to your Father in Heaven TODAY. Pray that He would give you a place in His Kingdom through faith in His Son Jesus.
4. Find a way to use every single one of your gifts and talents by serving others in a productive way at work, and church, and in the community. Find a way to serve the fatherless, visit the widows, and help the homeless and hospitalized.
5. Contact a Commandment Keeping Assembly of Believers in your city if you need to walk through receiving Salvation, Healing, Deliverance, or Discipleship! If you need help, please to go to http://www.h2h2hop.com.
6. Be faithful to your role in your family, your job, your congregation, your community, and in the kingdom of God. Become a good and faithful servant, knowing that your Father in Heaven is faithful to reward you.

GOD WILL RESTORE YOUR PLACE IN HIS KINGDOM

Even if you feel like you don't have a purpose, or have been misused, or violated in some way, you have the opportunity to be a productive and essential family member in relationship with the King of the whole earth!

You must repent to God, believe in Jesus, be forgiven of sin, and forgive others of their sin against you. You must be baptized in water, healed from brokenness, and delivered from demonic spirits from your past. You will be filled with the Spirit of God.

He will cover you and you will find out that you have been given tremendous gifts and a place in His Kingdom that only you can fill!

Chapter 10

RESTORING ALL THINGS

YAHUAH is a Father to the Fatherless!

Many of us have experienced different degrees of fatherlessness that have caused us to suffer loss in our souls, but God has sent the Spirit of Elijah to confront our idolatry, destroy our rebellion, rebuild true worship, and make way for Yahushua aka JESUS to bring healing, deliverance, salvation, and restoration to our hearts!

Here are the instructions from the Most High:

FATHERS: Turn your hearts away from Idolatry and Adultery, and back to God and Family!

CHILDREN: Forgive your fathers that did you wrong and submit to the 10 Commandments of your Father in Heaven!

> *Malachi 4:5 Behold, I will send you Elijah
> the prophet before the coming of the great and
> dreadful day of the Lord: 6 And he shall **turn
> the heart of the fathers to the children**, and*

the heart of the children to their fathers,
lest I come and smite the earth with a curse.

This is the way forward.

We all know it wasn't our fault that we were abused or abandoned or born into brokenness and violence…but eventually we all become responsible for our own character, integrity, and covenant faithfulness.

We must Repent. Believe in Jesus. Obey God's Commandments. Be Forgiven. Forgive others. Be healed. Be delivered from devils. Be discipled. Submit to Natural and Spiritual Order.

This is the Way forward!

This is the way to enter the Kingdom of God through His son. Repentance and Forgiveness can only be found in the Name of Jesus and the Love of our Father in Heaven.

> *Proverbs 30:11* **There is a generation** *that curseth*
> *their father, and doth not bless their mother.*
> *12* **There is a generation** *that are*
> *pure in their own eyes, and yet is not*
> *washed from their filthiness.*
> *13* **There is a generation***, O how lofty are*
> *their eyes! and their eyelids are lifted up.*
> *14* **There is a generation***, whose teeth are*
> *as swords, and their jaw teeth as knives,*
> *to devour the poor from off the earth,*
> *and the needy from among men.*

We Can Change this Direction in ONE Generation!

The antidote to fatherlessness will never be "making it", becoming rich, becoming a "giant" (aka Superstar) in the earth, or becoming known and influential.

If that's what your heart is searching for, your heart will always be fatherless.

The remedy for fatherlessness is becoming healed from your wounds, becoming obedient to Gods Word, becoming delivered from the iniquities of the devil, and becoming content in submission to the ways of your Father in Heaven.

This can only be done by imitating the Son of God who chased purity and obedience in His Father's Holy name.

You are Responsible for Loving God with Your Whole Soul

Those that had a tragic fatherhood are tempted to live in rebellion out of hurt, pain, and unforgiveness.

Those that were blessed with quality fathers are tempted to walk in rebellion just to be "cool" and fit into a rebellious culture out of pride.

Both will be judged, but whose judgement will be worse? The latter, of course, because they have been **given more**.

Jesus taught that those that have been **given much**, also have much **more required** of them (Luke 12:48). Jesus also taught that those that have been **forgiven much**, **give very much love** to God (Luke 7:47).

Ultimately, whether you have been **given much** or **forgiven much**, we all have to **give our lives to love and obey God** with our whole heart, soul, mind, and strength.

If you were blessed with a good earthly father, you are required to give your Heavenly Father **much more** obedient love and service.

If you were forgiven of your sins of rebellion when you met your Heavenly Father, then you must love your Heavenly Father **very much** by giving Him everything you have in obedience.

Follow the Father Above

We as the Body of Christ must have COMPASSION on the fatherless, but we must not FOLLOW after the fatherless or DWELL in any of our pain and rebellion.

We ALL must Forgive our earthly fathers, allow our hearts to Heal, and Learn how to follow our Father in Heaven, as dear children. Only YAH is the Father of Spirits, and He is the Giver of every good and perfect gift!

> *Psalms 68: [5] A **father of the fatherless**, and a judge of the widows, is God in his holy habitation. [6] God setteth the solitary in families: he bringeth out those which are bound with chains: but the rebellious dwell in a dry land.*

Get to know your ABBA FATHER in Heaven!

He has a VISION, a TESTIMONY, a STANDARD, and a PLAN.

He will RESTORE ALL THINGS!

TURN YOUR HEARTS TODAY!

Fathers, a prayer for you and your children:

> "Heavenly Father, please forgive me for the wrong I've done to you and to my family. Help me to forgive and be forgiven. Help me to learn your Commandments and do them, because your Commandments are not extreme, and they work

out the best for everyone. Help me to be saved by believing in the death and resurrection of your Son King Jesus to deliver me from my sins. I pray that my children would have mercy from you and that you would heal and restore their hearts. Please reconcile me with you, my covenant wife, and my children."

Children, a prayer for you and your earthly father:

"Heavenly Father, please forgive me for any ingratitude for the good things that you have done for me through my father and mother. Help me to forgive the errors and sins of my father so that I can also be forgiven by you and move forward in life. Please help me to reconcile and rebuild a relationship with my father on earth because all things are possible with you. Help me to be saved by believing in the death and resurrection of your Son King Jesus to deliver me from my sins. Teach me the wisdom of obeying your Commandments because they are not extreme, and they work out the best for everyone."

Malachi 4: 1 For, behold, the day cometh, that shall burn as an oven; and all the proud, yea, and all that do wickedly, shall be stubble: and the day that cometh shall burn them up, saith the Lord of hosts, that it shall leave them neither root nor branch.
2 But unto you that fear my name shall the Sun of righteousness arise with healing in his wings; and ye shall go forth, and grow up as calves of the stall.
3 And ye shall tread down the wicked; for they shall be ashes under the soles of your feet in the day that I shall do this, saith the Lord of hosts.

*4 Remember ye the law of Moses my servant,
which I commanded unto him in Horeb for
all Israel, with the statutes and judgments.
5 Behold, I will send you Elijah the
prophet before the coming of the great
and dreadful day of the Lord:
6 And he shall turn the heart of the
fathers to the children, and the heart of
the children to their fathers, lest I come
and smite the earth with a curse.*

"My God, my God, why have you forsaken me?"

Even as Jesus was bearing the sin of the world on the Tree of Calvary didn't complain about the nails, the blood, the beating.

What did he cry out about? The feeling of forsakenness from His Father.

Feeling unwanted, forsaken, or unloved by your father is the deepest pain that a person can ever feel.

Jesus Suffered More than You

Jesus suffered more Pain than you.

Jesus suffered more Trauma than you.

Jesus suffered more Rejection than you did.

Jesus was Despised and taken advantage of much more than you have been.

Why? Because Jesus did absolutely nothing wrong—yet He was beaten and killed to pay the price for people that still, to this day, don't respect or obey Him.

Jesus was forsaken by His own Father in His most Difficult Moment; He was abandoned.

Yes, Jesus cares about your story. He is here to help you recover, and conquer, and heal, and overcome.

However, your story is not better than His Story. On your Judgement Day, it will be too late to tell your story. You have to learn His Story now.

On your Judgement Day, you won't be able to make any excuses to the One who suffered more than you did.

He Suffered the Most!

Even though Jesus is the Son of God and the King of Kings, He still identifies with our suffering. Just because He is the Son of God doesn't mean He doesn't understand our pains. He suffered much more than we did.

Jesus is a suffering servant, but because He is also a sinless King, He retains the right to Judge us on the last day.

Here is what the One who Suffered the Most will Judge you for on Judgement Day:

1.   **You will be judged for your WORDS:**

     Matthew 12:36 But I say unto you, That EVERY IDLE WORD that men shall speak, they shall give account thereof in the day of judgment.

     37 For BY THY WORDS thou shalt be JUSTIFIED, and BY THY WORDS thou shalt be CONDEMNED.

2.   **You will be judged for your ACTIONS:**

     Revelation 2:19 I know THY WORKS, and charity, and service, and faith, and thy patience, and thy works; and the last to be more than the first.

Revelation 3:2 Be watchful, and strengthen the things which remain, that are ready to die: for I have not found THY WORKS perfect before God.

Revelation 20:12 And I saw the dead, the great and the small, standing before the throne, and books were opened; and another book was opened, which is the book of life; and the dead were JUDGED from the things which were written in the books, ACCORDING TO THEIR DEEDS.

2 Corinthians 5:10 For we must all appear before the JUDGMENT seat of Christ, so that each one may be RECOMPENSED for his DEEDS IN THE BODY, according to what he HAS DONE, whether GOOD or BAD.

3. **You will be judged for the TRUTH you HEARD but REJECTED and IGNORED:**

Matthew 12:47 And if any man HEAR MY WORDS, and BELIEVE NOT, I judge him not: for I came not to judge the world, but to save the world.

48 He that REJECTETH me, and RECEIVETH NOT MY WORDS, hath one that judgeth him: THE WORD THAT I HAVE SPOKEN, the same SHALL JUDGE HIM IN THE LAST DAYS.

This info on EXACTLY what we will be JUDGED ON comes DIRECTLY from Jesus the King and Judge of all of Us!

But the Good News is that He offers Forgiveness, Healing, and Deliverance for you if you Repent from Sin and Obey Him.

More Good News is that He not only tells us what we will be JUDGED by, He tells us EXACTLY HOW TO PASS THE TEST OF JUDGEMENT!

HERE IS HOW YOU CAN PASS YOUR JUDGEMENT DAY TEST:

1. Repent to God: TURN AWAY from your sinful ways and thoughts, and Keep God's 10 Commandments.
2. Believe in and Obey Jesus the King: The Son of God's Death, Burial, and Resurrection gave you the opportunity to get FORGIVENESS and SALVATION from your sins.
3. Get Baptized in Water: For your NEW LIFE and your New Beginning.
4. Pray for an Overflow of the Holy Spirit: Receive the POWER TO OBEY God, Demonstrate, and Tell others everything you have seen and heard about Jesus.
5. Be Taught and DISCIPLED in the Scriptures.
6. CONNECT with a Commandment keeping Assembly of Believers.
7. LISTEN to God's Voice and OBEY God daily.

CALL OUT TO YOUR ABBA FATHER FOR SALVATION:

"Father, forgive me for sinning against your commandments. I believe that your Son Jesus was punished by shedding His innocent blood; not for His sins, but for mine. I thank you for your mercy on me and I promise to follow and obey You all the days of my life. Amen."

If you would like to connect with our ministry in real life or receive free Kingdom discipleship training, please go to www.h2h2hop.com

---